The Open University

Humanities: A Foundation Course *Unit L1*

Introduction to Logic

Parts I to IX

Prepared by Susan Wilson for the Arts Foundation Course Team

THE OPEN UNIVERSITY PRESS

The Open University Press
Walton Hall Bletchley
Buckinghamshire.

First published 1971. Reprinted 1971

Designed by The Media Development Group of The Open University.

Printed in Great Britain by
EYRE AND SPOTTISWOODE LTD.
AT GROSVENOR PRESS PORTSMOUTH
SBN 335 00520 9

Open University courses provide a method of study for independent learners through an integrated teaching system, including textual material, radio and television programmes and short residential courses. This text is one of a series that make up the correspondence element of the Arts Foundation course.

For general availability of supporting material referred to in this text, please write to the Director of Marketing, The Open University, Walton Hall, Bletchley, Buckinghamshire.

Further information on Open University courses may be obtained from The Admissions Office, The Open University, P.O. Box 48, Bletchley, Buckinghamshire.

1.2

Contents

~T = F
~F = T

T & F = T
T & F = F
F & T = F
F & F = F

T v T = T
T v F = T
F v T = T
F v F = F

T → T = T
T → F = F
F → T = T
F → F = T

Part I

I Introduction

What is logic, and why should one study it? In the space of this short introduction, I can do no more than sketch answers to these two questions. You will discover what logic is as you go through the course. My main aim now is to explain why we have thought it a good idea to include some logic in our Foundation Course; but in order to do this, I have to indicate roughly what logic is, for those of you who may have only a hazy idea of its nature.

What is logic?

So first, what is logic? One answer is: the science of argument. But this is not very enlightening; we must explain first, what we mean by argument, and then perhaps also what we mean by a science. One might make a first shot at explaining what one normally means by an argument by saying something like this: when two people are arguing, one is trying to convince the other that something is true or that something is false. But there are many ways of doing this, not all of which involve logic. You may for instance persuade a man to believe something by appealing to his emotions, or to intuition: by saying things like "In your heart you know he's right"—one of Barry Goldwater's campaign slogans. Or you may attack his own beliefs with ridicule or derision: "If you'll believe that you'll believe anything". Or you may bear down on him by the sheer force of your own conviction or authority: "You mark my words, I know what I'm talking about". Quite often, when two people are having an argument, something like this is going on. But this is not what we mean by an argument when we call logic "the science of argument". An argument, in the logical sense, attempts not just to convince you that some statement is true by whatever means comes to mind, but provides good grounds for the truth of that statement. Logic is the study of these good grounds. We can see what this means if we consider a logical argument in more detail. Such an argument consists typically of one or more statements called "premisses", and a further statement called the "conclusion". The conclusion is the statement whose truth or falsity is in dispute. An argument is sound, or valid, when its premisses do constitute good grounds for its conclusion. In this case we say that the conclusion follows from, or is the consequence of, its premisses. An argument is unsound, or invalid, when its premisses do not constitute good grounds for its conclusion. In this case we say the conclusion does not follow from its premisses. Logic is the science of what follows from what: the science of the relation between premisses and conclusion. This might be called the *consequence relation.*

You may doubt that anything imposing enough to be called a science could be constructed round the consequence relation. But it is trickier and more complicated than it seems. For instance, it soon becomes clear that we seem to use two different kinds of consequence relation in real-life arguments, and these two kinds of consequence relation seem to distinguish two different kinds of logic. Sometimes we want to say that a conclusion follows from its premisses, if the truth of the premisses guarantees the truth of the conclusion: if the premisses are true then the conclusion cannot but be true, or the argument contradicts itself. The study of this kind of relation is called **deductive logic.** An example of deductive argument is that old philosophical favourite, "All men are mortal, Socrates is a man, therefore Socrates is mortal". If it is true that all men are mortal, and it is true that Socrates is a man, we cannot avoid the conclusion that Socrates is mortal. However, we may often feel that one statement provides good grounds for another without absolutely guaranteeing its truth in this way. Suppose, for example, it were true that every man who had ever smoked a cigarette had died of lung cancer. You would be inclined to regard this as a good reason for believing that the next man to smoke a cigarette would also die of lung cancer. In other words you would be inclined to regard the argument "Every man who has ever smoked a cigarette has died of lung cancer, therefore the next man to smoke a cigarette will die of lung cancer" as sound. But it is easy enough to imagine the premiss true and the conclusion false: the next man to smoke a cigarette might get knocked down by a bus before he had a chance to die of lung cancer. The truth of the premisses does not guarantee the truth of the conclusion. The study of this kind of argument is called **inductive logic.**

Deductive logic

Inductive logic

Exercise: Read through this section, "What is logic?" once more. Now see if you can write down, in your own words and without referring to the text again, a brief description of what logic is and the difference between deductive and inductive logic.

Your logic course, and what we hope you will get out of it.

Most of this course is devoted to deductive logic: only the last few sections are concerned with inductive logic. This is because deductive logic as a technique or science is far more highly developed than inductive logic. One reason for this is that there is general agreement among philosophers and logicians about the basic rules and principles of deductive logic; but this is not the case with inductive logic. I do not mean by this that in the case of inductive logic, there is disagreement about which arguments are sound and which are unsound: everyone accepts and rejects the same types of argument, but there is much controversy over what exactly it is about these types of argument that *makes* them sound or unsound. This controversy has hindered the development of inductive logic. In striking contrast, however, has been the progress of deductive logic: during this century and the last there have been tremendous advances in this field. The state of the field now might be compared to the state of physics after Newton or mathematics after Descartes, or indeed to the current state of molecular biology, with the discovery of the structure of DNA. Modern deductive logic is an expanding and exciting discipline, more akin to mathematics than to anything else, as you will see. In fact some of its greatest early practitioners (Bertrand Russell, for instance) developed it specifically in order to solve the philosophical problem of the foundations of mathematics. (Russell hoped to show that the whole of mathematics was in fact a branch of logic). In this aspect, logic has made major contributions to mathematics, for example to the theory of computers. However, since deductive logic has developed recently in mathematical contexts, it is not very well adapted for the analysis of any ordinary argument which you are likely to encounter. This is *not* because the deductive logic used in ordinary arguments is fundamentally different from deductive logic as used by a professional logician: it is because in ordinary argument we use such a very small part (and, from the point of view of the logician, such a very uninteresting part) of the sophisticated apparatus now available. You will in fact only be studying a tiny corner of this apparatus; those of you who are not mathematically inclined need not be alarmed at the prospect. But I hope it will be enough to give you some idea of the nature of the subject, and perhaps for some of you to develop a taste for it for its own sake. So this is one reason for including deductive logic in the Foundation Course: to introduce a recent and exciting human achievement which will be unfamiliar to most of you.

It is quite possible, however, that this particular kind of subject just will not appeal to you. If this is so, why should you study it? What is there in it for you? This brings me to one of the most fascinating aspects of logic. A few years ago we used to hear a lot about the "two cultures"—the traditional, literary culture and the new mathematical culture of the scientist—and the lack of communication between the two. Logic is unique in that it spans *both* cultures; it has one foot in mathematics and one in philosophy. Nowadays some acquaintance with elementary logic is regarded as part of the basic equipment of the academic philosopher. This is hardly surprising: logic is the study of arguments, and the business of a philosopher is to construct valid arguments in support of his views (which other philosophers who disagree with him will then do their utmost to show are invalid.) The development of modern logic has provided many philosophers with a source of inspiration: with new ways of constructing arguments and new ways of attacking philosophical problems. On the other hand, there are also many philosophers who view the influence of modern logic on philosophy with deep suspicion. The whole area is one of heated controversy. You can therefore regard this logic course as part of your introduction to philosophy. There is in fact a fair amount of philosophy in it; I have not stressed this aspect, but I have tried to give some indication in the text of the places where I raise *philosophical*, as opposed to specifically *logical* questions. So an additional reason for studying logic as part of an Humanities Foundation Course is because elementary logic is part of the groundwork of philosophy. However, let us now suppose the worst: suppose you turn out to loathe equally both logic and philosophy. In this case, is there still any reason why you should study either of them? It is usually of doubtful value to struggle grimly with a subject that has no interest at all for you; but nevertheless, I think there is a case for persevering at least for a while with both philosophy and logic. It is, I'm afraid, the reason usually put forward for undergoing experiences not entirely to one's taste: namely, that it will probably be good for you. The study of logic provides a training in analysis which should help you in your appraisal of arguments in ordinary life, and will certainly help you in your appraisal of arguments in philosophy. The proper appraisal of arguments must be of vital concern to everybody. Rational decisions require rational appraisal of the arguments for doing one thing, or accepting one view, rather than another. The value of the course in this sphere lies not so much in detailed instruction or rules of thumb, but in developing the analytical habit of mind and suggesting an ideal standard of proof. Arguments in real life are seldom either well-constructed or well laid out; logic will teach you what a really watertight argument should look like, and provide a standard of comparison for arguments in real life. Both the deductive and the inductive parts of the course should be useful to you here; though in neither case will it be perhaps in quite the direct way you might expect.

You will find that deductive logic will give you quite precise and unambiguous rules for conducting arguments; but you may not be able to apply these rules to real arguments in ordinary language very often or very easily. On the other hand, you will scarcely find an ordinary argument that does not use inductive rules somewhere; but the rules of inductive logic are of their nature imprecise and difficult to formulate—so it seems at the present state of our knowledge at any rate—so that though you may constantly be wishing to apply them, you may well be unsure what exactly it is you are trying to apply. It is all very unfortunate; but after all, we have no right to expect the discovery of truth to be an easy matter. In the last resort, it is up to you to use what you learn as best you can.

Practical details: how to use the correspondence text

Programmed learning A large part of the course will proceed by programmed learning methods. This means that every now and then as you read through the text you will be required to make an active response: to answer a question, complete a sentence, or some such thing. The signal that a response is expected of you is a solid line across the page. I shall call this line a **response-line.** The portion of text between the response-lines, and before the first and after the last response-line of each part, is called a **frame.** As you read through the text, cover up everything below the first frame or part of a frame on each page: that is, cover up everything below the first response-line on the page. (We have given you a special card for this purpose). When you reach the response-line, stop and make the required response; write your answer in the right-hand margin. The correct answer is printed in the right-hand margin just below the response-line, and should be covered by your card. Only when you have written down your answer should you move the card down to the next response-line, check your answer, and go on to read the next frame. DON'T CHEAT: you will get no credit for making the right responses in the text, and if you cheat you will only hinder your own learning. As an additional safeguard against your seeing the answers accidentally, we have printed them in smaller type to make them less conspicuous.

Response-line

Frame

The questions which occur in the text are simply *teaching* devices; they are meant to ram points home, rather than to test your understanding. That is why they have deliberately been made very easy:

you are expected to get nearly all (90%) right. If you get three or more in a row wrong, this will be a sign that there is something you have not understood: re-read the preceding part of the text carefully, and don't go on until you have understood your mistake. DO NOT READ THROUGH THE TEXT WITHOUT MAKING THE REQUIRED RESPONSES. If you do this, you will lose all the benefit of this kind of teaching.

The text is divided into eighteen parts. At the end of some parts you will find a set of exercises; these are included so that you can yourself test your understanding of the preceding part. Answers to the exercises are given on the page immediately following them. Do as many of the exercises as it takes to convince you that you have thoroughly understood the preceding part: ideally you should continue doing them until you effortlessly get them all right. Sometimes different groups of exercises test different things from a particular part: in this case you should do at least some of each group. You will not be assessed on your performance on these exercises. They are provided to help you assimilate the material and check up on your own progress.

Definitions When important technical terms which you should remember appear for the first time in the text, they are printed in bold face and in black **like this.** The terms are repeated in the same type in the right-hand margin, opposite the place where they are defined. (You will see an example of this on p. 4, where I have defined 'response-line' and 'frame'.) We have done this to highlight the technical terms and help you find the definitions again if you should need them.

Numbering Each of the parts of the logic course is numbered, from I to XVIII (1 to 18). The part-number occurs in Roman numerals at the beginning of each part. In the programmed parts of the text (i.e. the parts containing response-lines) the frames are also numbered (remember, the frames are the portions of the text between the response-lines). Frame numbers appear in the *left-hand* margin, in ordinary Arabic numerals. A new sequence of frame-numbers is started with each part: that is, the first frame of each part is numbered 1. Frames will sometimes be referred to by both part- and frame-numbers: 'Frame IV 25' means frame 25 of part IV; 'X 25' means frame 25 of part X. Some sections (for example this one!) contain no response-lines, and hence no frames or frame numbers. Examples to which frequent reference is made in the text are also numbered, thus: Ex 8. This means: Example 8. The sequence of example numbers is continuous throughout the course: a new sequence is *not* started with each new part. You will receive parts 1–9 and parts 10–18 of the course in two separate packages.

Planning your work Logic is not a typical Arts subject. I said earlier that it was like mathematics; now, while the Arts student works by writing essays, the Maths student works by doing calculations or solving problems. Much of the work you do in logic will be a kind of calculation—something like verbal algebra. We thought we should take account of this in planning the Foundation Course. Most of the Arts units come to you in study blocks of two to four weeks;

you are asked to study each unit by concentrated work on it during the weeks of that study block. However, most people unaccustomed to mathematical work would find it very taxing indeed to master, say, algebra, by concentrated work over a short time on algebra alone. For this sort of reason we have decided to spread the logic course over several weeks, so that you can work on it in parallel with other subjects. We have allowed an hour a week for logic, and expect you to need on average about an hour to complete each of the 18 parts of the logic course; so we expect you to have completed all 18 parts by the end of the first 18 weeks of the year. You should start work on logic straight away. Assignments will be set on the assumption that you are completing at least one part of the logic course each week.

It is important to work through the sections in the proper order. You will not be able to understand the later sections if you have not worked through the preceding sections first.

General descriptions of parts I–IX All the nine parts in this package are concerned with deductive logic. The goal of the deductive part of this course is to show you that there exists a systematic method of calculating whether arguments of a particular kind are valid or not. But before you can start systematically evaluating arguments, you must thoroughly master the system which makes such evaluations possible. Parts I–IX are entirely concerned with setting up this system (I–V, IX) and explaining its relation to ordinary language (VI-VIII). In this first part of the course, your main task will be to master this system, that is essentially to learn a new language; but the purpose for which you are learning it will not yet fully emerge. This will come in the second half of the course: so you must get perfectly fluent in the new language before the second logic package arrives. Practically all of the exercises in I–IX are designed largely to familiarise you with this language; once you have got the hang of it, you should be able to do the exercises very quickly and easily, indeed almost mechanically. But do not despise them on that account: remember that what you are aiming at is such perfect familiarity with the language that what was at first an exercise demanding care and thought becomes a response which is almost second nature. Ideally you should be able to do correctly exercises such as those in parts IV, V and IX (these are the parts concerned with setting up the system in detail) almost without thinking. If you master these first nine parts thoroughly, it will pay you great dividends in increased speed and ease of comprehension in the second half of the course.

Assessment In the course of the year you will receive two logic assignments; your performance on these will count towards your final assessment for the logic component of the Foundation Course. Instructions will be included with the assignments.

Further reading

There are no prescribed books for the logic course. However, I have suggested a few titles in case you should want to read around the subject. Whether you do any extra reading or not is entirely up to you: the correspondence course is self-sufficient. It has not been based on any existing text-book, and there is no book to which you can easily refer for direct help with it. Obviously, however, if you do read any of the books described below, your general grasp of the subject will be broadened and deepened.

Logic, Wesley C. Salmon. A very straightforward general introduction, suitable for the reader with no background in logic or philosophy. This is a book to read straight through once to get an overall picture of the subject—particularly if what you are mainly interested in is the relevance of logic to ordinary life and language.

Introduction to Logic and to the Methodology of Deductive Sciences, Alfred Tarski. An elementary text by one of the greatest of modern logicians. Don't be put off by the terrifying title. This is an introduction to the whole field of modern mathematical logic, and will appeal if you are interested in the technical mathematical aspect of the subject. Chapter II covers much the same ground as our course. Tarski uses a different notation from ours; but if you are seriously interested in logic, you had better get used to this—there is a vast variety of different notations in use.

Introduction to Logic: the Criticism of Arguments, Peter Alexander.* Another general introduction, coming somewhere between Salmon and Tarski in approach. Unlike Tarski, Alexander approaches logic from the ordinary language, rather than from the mathematical end; but he does pay more attention to the technical aspects than does Salmon, and is very much more thorough. Probably the best introductory text of the three for the really serious general reader. Again, slightly different notation from both ours and Tarski's.

The remaining books are all technical texts for the serious student of logic, and are not primarily intended or suitable for the general reader. All go at least ten times as fast as our correspondence course: this is no exaggeration, and may be an understatement. All cover very much more ground than is covered by the correspondence course. Nevertheless, parts of them could be both interesting and useful to you, taken in conjunction with the correspondence course, as I have tried to indicate below. You may in any case like to see what the real stuff looks like!

Elementary Logic, Benson Mates. This is a difficult and technical book which I recommend entirely for the sake of chapters 1, 2 and 12. Chapter 1 is an account of the basic principles of logic, and almost amounts to a ground-plan of our course. If you find it difficult to keep a sense of direction as you work through the details of the programmed text, it may help you to read through the excellent summary in chapter 1 of Mates just *because* it goes about ten times as fast as our course. Chapter 2 is less directly relevant to our course, but worth reading nevertheless. Chapter 12 is an interesting account of the history of logic.

Methods of Logic, W. V. O. Quine. A basic text by an eminent logician and philosopher. I include it because Quine alone of these technical authors pays considerable attention to translation. The introduction and Part I (especially §1–§8) can be read with profit; you can skip the technical bits. A different notation again.

---

*Unfortunately this book, which was only recently published by Allen & Unwin, came to my notice too late to be included in the "recommended books" list for 1971, which the University circulated to the public libraries; so some of you may have difficulty in getting hold of it.

Beginning Logic, E. J. Lemmon. I love this book. Try it. It is an elementary technical text which I include in case you should really want to try your hand at formal logic. It is not as difficult as the book by Mates, and if you are keen you should be able to manage at least the early part of it. Lemmon's approach is quite different from mine: let me stress that I recommend this book for interest and enjoyment only—don't read it to get help with the correspondence course.

Part II

II Basic Principles

if **p**

q then

Part II

II Basic principles: deduction, statements, arguments.

What is deduction?

1 In this section I am going to try and explain what deductive logic is. In fact the best way of finding out what deduction is, is to do some: but a few introductory remarks may be useful, to lead you into the subject, and give you some idea of how it may be relevant to your interests.

We all use deduction all the time, though often we may hardly notice it. Consider this common English expression:

If Stalin was a Communist, then I'm a Dutchman.

This is not meant to be taken literally; one uses this particular idiom as a roundabout way of saying

Stalin was not a Communist.

Similarly,

If Kipling was a poet then I'm a Dutchman

would be a roundabout way of saying

Kipling was not a poet

2 How do we get from the statement that we say—

If Stalin was a Communist, then I'm a Dutchman

or

If Kipling was a poet then I'm a Dutchman

to the statement that we mean to convey—

Stalin was not a Communist

or

Kipling was not a poet?

How does this particular idiom work—that is, convey the message it is intended to convey?

The first thing to notice is that, where a person uses this expression in the normal way, though he only says *one* thing—

If Stalin was a Communist, then I'm a Dutchman

he expects his hearer to understand something else as well—namely

I am not a Dutchman.

Similarly, if one wanted to convey "Kipling was not a poet" by using this idiom, the statement one would *say* would be

---

3 and the statement one would expect to be understood, without it being said, would be

If Kipling was a poet, then I'm a Dutchman

---

4 Now, from this pair of statements

If Stalin was a Communist then I'm a Dutchman
I am not a Dutchman

I am not a Dutchman

there follows logically a third statement. This statement is

Stalin was not a Communist.

And this third statement is the one that the idiom "If Stalin was a Communist, then I'm a Dutchman" is used to convey.

Similarly, from the pair of statements

If Kipling was a poet then I'm a Dutchman
I'm not a Dutchman

there follows logically the third statement

---

5 It may not be immediately obvious to you that

Kipling was not a poet

Stalin was not a Communist

Kipling was not a poet

follow logically from

If Stalin was a Communist, then I'm a Dutchman
I am not a Dutchman

and

If Kipling was a poet then I'm a Dutchman
I am not a Dutchman

respectively. In any case, what exactly do we mean by "follows logically"? These things may become clearer if we look at some more examples. Consider these two statements:

If this liquid is an acid, it turns blue litmus paper red.
It does not turn blue litmus paper red.

What would you conclude, if someone told you these two things?

---

6 Or supposing someone told you the following two things:

It (this liquid) is not an acid

If the note was typed on the office typewriter, then the e's in the text are smudged.
The e's in the text are not smudged
What would you conclude?

---

7 Let's take another look at the four examples we have had so far, put next to each other:

Ex. 1. *If Stalin was a Communist, then I'm a Dutchman.*
I am not a Dutchman.
Therefore, Stalin was not a Communist.

Ex. 2. *If Kipling was a poet, then I'm a Dutchman.*
I am not a Dutchman.
Therefore, Kipling was not a poet.

Ex. 3. *If this liquid is an acid, then it turns blue litmus paper red.*
It does not turn blue litmus paper red.
Therefore, it is not an acid.

Ex. 4. *If the note was typed on the office typewriter, then the e's in the text are smudged.*
The e's in the text are not smudged.
Therefore, the note was not typed on the office typewriter.

All these four examples have some features in common. First, how many statements are there in each?

The note was not typed on the office typewriter

---

8 There are two words, and two words only, which occur in the *first* statement of all four examples. What are they?

Three

---

9 There is one word, and one word only, which occurs in the *second* statement of all four examples. What is it?

If, then.

---

10 There are two words, and two words only, which occur in the *third* statement of all four examples. What are they?

Not

---

11 Look again at Ex. 1. The first line consists of two complete sentences (each of which is also a statement)—"Stalin was a Communist" and "I'm a Dutchman"—joined together by "if . . . then . . ." to make a new statement:

If [Stalin was a Communist] —then [I'm a Dutchman]

This is one of the standard ways in English of making new statements out of old, so to speak; different "If . . . then . . ." statements can be constructed by changing the statements in the two boxes in the diagram above. If we change the statement in the first box, "Stalin was a Communist", to the statement "Kipling was a poet", we obtain a new "If . . . then . . ." statement—our Ex. 2, "If Kipling was a poet, then I'm a Dutchman".

Therefore, not.

Let us give the name "p" to any statement in the "if" box, and the name "q" to any statement in the "then" box:

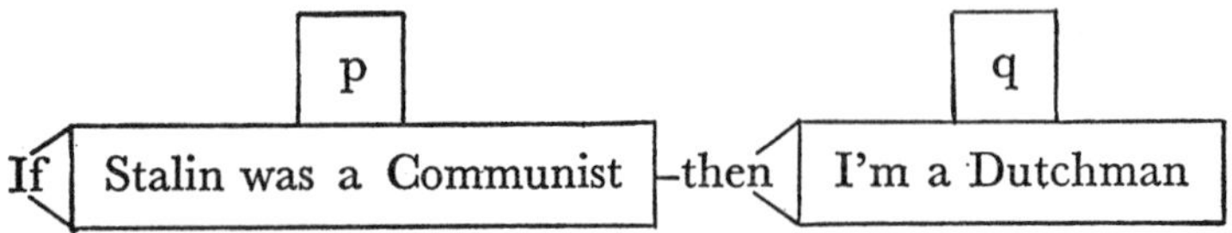

We can now say that the first line of Ex. 1 *can be represented by*, or has the **logical form,**

Logical form

If p, then q

Now look at the first line of Ex. 3. Which would be statement p—the statement in the "if" box?

---

12 Which would be statement q—the statement in the "then" box?

This liquid is an acid

---

13 How could we represent, or what is the logical form of, the first line of Ex. 3?

It turns blue litmus paper red.

---

14 Now look at the second line of Ex. 1. It is

If p, then q

I am not a Dutchman.

This looks like a whole new statement. But this is just due to one of the peculiarities of English grammar: it is just the denial of statement q in the first line, and if we form the negative in a different way, by putting "It is not the case that . . . " at the beginning of the sentence, instead of inserting "not" after the verb, we can see that like line 1, we can think of it as a new statement formed out of an old one by adding something on the front:

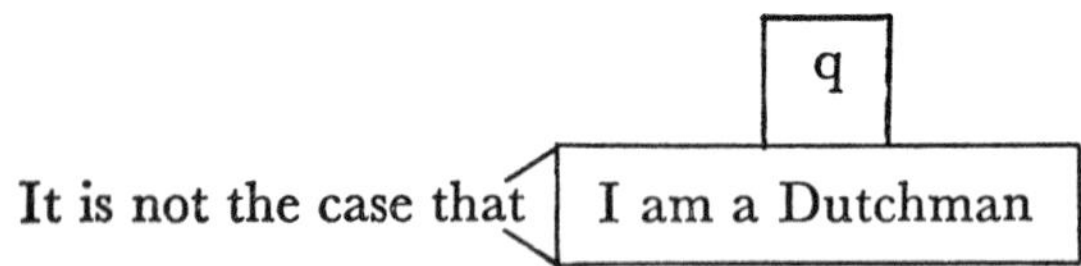

We can represent this by, or say it has the logical form:

Not q.

Similarly, the third statement of Ex. 1. is the denial or negation of sentence p in the first statement:

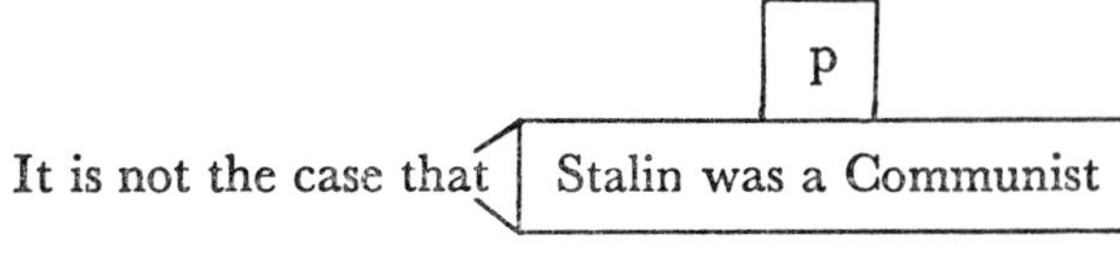

We can say that it has the form:

Not p.

So the whole argument of Ex. 1 has the logical form:

If p, then q
Not q
Therefore, not p

Using the same notation—that is, putting "p" for the sentence immediately following "if", and "q" for the sentence immediately following "then", and using Ex. 1 above as a model, how would you represent Ex. 2?

---

15 How would you represent Ex. 3?

If p, then q
Not q
Therefore, not p

---

16 How would you represent Ex. 4?

If p, then q
Not q
Therefore, not p

---

17 We can see that what all four examples have in common is that they *can all be represented in the same way*, or *have the same form*. It is clear that in each case the third statement follows from the other two purely by virtue of the logical form of the three statements involved: that is, by virtue of the meaning of "if . . . then . . ." and "not". The content and meaning of the sentences which are substituted for p and q are quite irrelevant to the argument: no matter what sentence you put for p and q, (provided that once you have decided what to put for p, you put the same sentence for p each time p occurs, and similarly for q) a statement of the form "not p" will always follow from two statements of the forms "if p, then q" and "not q".

If p, then q
Not q
Therefore, not p

There are a few basic logical terms in normal use (such as "if . . . then . . ." and "not"). The study of deduction is the study of these terms, and the study of which statements containing them follow from which. It is by using deductive logic that we are able to understand the message "Stalin was not a Communist" when we hear the idiom "If Stalin was a Communist, then I'm a Dutchman". It is because we all do deduction in our heads without noticing it that such an idiom is comprehensible to us. But, equally, since our logical processes often go unnoticed, they may often go *wrong* unnoticed too—especially when the argument gets more complicated than the very simple examples we have been considering. So conscious awareness of the rules we all use unconsciously may be an advantage. Logicians do not arbitrarily invent rules or legislate our thinking for us; on the whole they try to make explicit and clear the rules which are implicit in ordinary thinking.

One final point. We have talked a lot about sentences and sentence formation, and it may seem to you that what has been discussed is grammar rather than logic. Perhaps you feel that these rules, which I claim are logical rules, are really just rules about the use of English, and might be different in other languages. It is true that in order to understand logical concepts you need to be able to make some basic grammatical distinctions; for instance, you need to know what a *sentence* is. But logic is concerned with connections between sentences which are *not* grammatical connections; it is concerned with whether one sentence *follows from* another, regardless of whatever grammatical or linguistic device may be used to join the two together. The logic of an argument does not depend on the language in which the argument is expressed: logicians who speak different languages do not find that this makes them disagree about the rules of logic, or about the basic logical "operators" (such as "not" and "if—then")—even though these may be expressed linguistically in very different ways. If this linguistic doubt still worries you, perhaps it is worth remembering that the systematic study of logic started with Aristotle, who wrote in Greek—but this has not made his work inapplicable in English. The logic described by Aristotle has since expanded, but it has not fundamentally changed, no matter what the language of its later practitioners.

Statements

18 We have said that logic is the study of which statements follow from which. Before going any further, we must make clear what we mean by a "statement".

People use language for all sorts of purposes besides making statements: for giving commands, asking questions, exclaiming, cursing, even sometimes as a way of performing an action. For example, "Have you put the cat out?" is a *question.* "Don't put your daughter on the stage, Mrs. Worthington" is a *command.* "What a lovely day!" is an *exclamation.* "With this ring I thee wed" is (part of) a way of performing an action—in this case marrying someone. Call it a *performative.* But "The candidate is a conservationist" is a **statement.** **Statement**
What distinguishes statements from non-statements is that they can be true or false: neither questions, commands, exclamations, nor performatives can be true or false. If I say "What a lovely day!" when there is rain, hail, murk and freezing fog, my exclamation is inappropriate, not untrue. Again, we would not quite know what to make of a wedding guest who leapt up shouting "That's not true!" as the bridegroom was saying "With this ring I thee wed"—though we would know quite well what he meant if he shouted instead "Stop the ceremony!" or "The ceremony is void!" Performatives, however, are sometimes particularly tricky to distinguish from statements; unlike other non-statements, they are not usually distinguishable from statements by their grammatical form. "With these hands I did it" is no different grammatically speaking from "With this ring I thee wed", but the former is a statement and the latter is not. When in doubt always ask yourself: Would it be possible, or appropriate, to ask "Is that true?". If it is possible, your sentence is a statement.

Here are some examples for you to try your hand on. Delete the incorrect answers:

The people's flag is deepest red
is a
statement/command/question/exclamation

---

19 *It shrouded oft our martyred dead* Statement
is a
statement/command/question/exclamation

---

20 *And ere their limbs grew stiff and cold*
Their hearts' blood stained its every fold
is a
statement/command/question/exclamation

Statement

---

21 *Then raise the scarlet standard high*
is a
statement/command/question/exclamation

Statement

---

22 *Beneath its shade we'll live or die*
is either a statement or a kind of declaration of intent, depending on whether you take "we'll" (we will) as a simple future or as expressing a wish. If you take it as a simple future the line is a statement/not a statement.

Command

---

23 *Let cowards flinch and traitors sneer*
is a
statement/command/question/exclamation
(two possibilities)

A statement

---

24 *We'll keep the red flag flying here*
Taking "we'll" as a simple future,
this is
a statement/not a statement

Command/exclamation

---

25 How many statements in

God save our gracious Queen
Long live our noble Queen
God save the Queen
Send her victorious
Happy and glorious
Long to reign over us
God save the Queen

A statement

---

26 The sort of logic we are going to study is concerned only with statements. The National Anthem would therefore be of no interest to us as logicians. This is no reflection on the National Anthem! It is just intended to remind you that there are large and important areas of life and language about which the logician has little to say.

There are more complex kinds of statements and non-statements than the ones we have just been considering. For example, I said in the previous section on deduction (pages 11–16) that one of the standard

None

ways in English of making new statements out of old was to slot different statements into the "if" and "then" boxes of "if... then..." sentences. But not all "if... then..." sentences express statements; we only obtain a statement out of an "if... then..." sentence if we put statements into both of its two boxes, thus:

Ex. 5. If [this liquid is an acid] then [it turns blue litmus paper red.]

If instead we put questions, commands or exclamations into the boxes, we obtain either something which does not make sense, e.g.:

Ex. 6. If [is this liquid an acid] then [it turns blue litmus paper red.]

or something which is not a statement, e.g.:

Ex. 7. If [this liquid is an acid] then [why doesn't it turn blue litmus paper red?]

Ex. 6 does not make sense because we have put a question instead of a statement into the "if" box.
Ex. 7 is a question, because though there is a statement in the "if" box, the sentence in the "then" box is a question and this turns the whole sentence into a question.

Is the following example a statement?

If [you want to know the time] then [ask a policeman.]

---

27 Why not? — No

---

28 Is the following sentence a statement? — The sentence in the "then" box is not a statement but a command

If you don't want the whelks, don't muck 'em about.

---

29 Is the following sentence a statement? — No

If Stalin was a Communist, then Trotsky was a traitor.

---

30 Is the following sentence a statement? — Yes

Ex. 8. *If Stalin was a Communist, then was Trotsky a traitor?*

---

31 Why not? — No

Question

32 What is Ex. 8, if it is not a statement?

The sentence after the "then" is not a statement but a question

---

33 Is the following example a statement?

If Stalin was a Communist, then Trotsky

A question

No

Not a sentence

34 Why not?

No

---

35 Is the following example a statement?

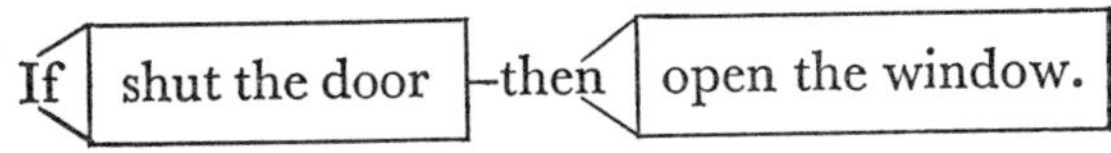

It does not make sense: what follows the "then" is not a complete sentence

No

---

if sent command
then sent command

36 Why not?

No

---

37 Arguments

Logicians study arguments. In this section we shall learn what arguments are, and what their various parts are called.

Logicians are concerned with which statements follow from which. They therefore frequently consider groups of statements with the object of seeing if any of them follow from the others. A group of statements considered in this way is called an **argument.**

We must not confuse an argument in the logical sense—a group of statements considered from the point of view of whether any of them follow from the others—with an argument in the other, perhaps more normal sense, of something like a quarrel. Let us distinguish the "quarrel" sense of "argument" by calling it a "dispute". Whenever we use the word "argument", we shall mean an argument in the *logical* sense. Not all disputes are arguments. For instance consider the conversation below:

Ex. 9. *1st speaker:* "Your father's not as tall as my father!"
2nd speaker: "Yes, he is!"
1st speaker: "No, he isn't!"
2nd speaker: "Yes, he is!"
1st speaker: "No, he isn't!"
. . . etc.

This conversation contains just two statements about the second speaker's father: one says that he is not as tall as the first speaker's father, the other that he is. But since each speaker simply asserts his statement, without providing any further statements for it to follow from, the conversation is *not* an argument, though it is a dispute. But consider this example:

It does not make sense; the sentence in the "if" box is a command, and so is the sentence in the "then" box.

Argument

Ex. 10. *1st speaker:* "My father's taller than your father!"
2nd speaker: "No, he's not!"
1st speaker: "Yes he is, he's 6 ft. 2 ins. tall. Your father's only 6 ft. 1 in.!"

How many different statements does the first speaker produce?

---

38 Does any of these statements follow from the others?

Three

---

39 Which is the statement that follows from the others?

Yes

---

40 Which are the statements that it follows from?

My father's taller than your father.

---

41 Does the first speaker produce an argument in the logical sense?

My father's 6ft. 2ins. tall.
Your father's only 6ft. 1in.

---

42 An argument divides naturally into two parts. The statement (statements) which *follows* is called the **conclusion** (conclusions). All other statements are called **premisses** (singular **premiss**).

Yes
Conclusion
Premiss

In the argument:

If this liquid is an acid, then it turns blue litmus paper red.
It does not turn blue litmus paper red.
It is not an acid.

the statement

If this liquid is an acid, then it turns blue litmus paper red

is a

premiss/~~conclusion~~
(delete the incorrect answer).

---

43 And the statement:

Premiss

It does not turn blue litmus paper red

is a

premiss/~~conclusion~~.

---

44 And the statement

Premiss

It is not an acid

is a

~~premiss~~/conclusion

---

45 What are the premisses of the argument in Ex. 10? (page 20)

Conclusion

---

46 What is the conclusion of the argument in Ex. 10?

"He's (my father) 6ft. 2ins."
and "Your father's only 6ft. 1in."

---

47 Sometimes the conclusion of one argument is the premiss of another:

My father's taller than your father.

Ex. 11. *All moorhens have large green feet*
Magnus is a moorhen
Magnus has large, green feet
Magnus is a bird
At least one bird has large, green feet.

If we take "Magnus has large green feet" as a conclusion, what are the two premisses from which it follows?

---

48 If we take "At least one bird has large, green feet" as a conclusion, what are the premisses from which it follows?

All moorhens have large green feet
Magnus is a moorhen.

---

49 We will now introduce some conventions for writing out arguments in ordinary language, to help us see at a glance which are premisses and which are conclusions.

Magnus has large, green feet
Magnus is a bird.

We will write all the premisses first, with each separate premiss on a new line:

All moorhens have large, green feet
Magnus is a moorhen

We will draw a horizontal dotted line under the last premiss, and write the conclusion under it:

All moorhens have large, green feet
Magnus is a moorhen

....

Magnus has large, green feet.

Anything that appears *above* the dotted line is a premiss.
Anything that appears *below* the dotted line is a conclusion from the premisses above the line.
This means that you *cannot* write out the two arguments in Ex. 11 like this:

All moorhens have large, green feet
Magnus is a moorhen

....

Magnus has large, green feet
Magnus is a bird

....

At least one bird has large, green feet

unless you mean to suggest that "Magnus is a bird" is a conclusion from the two premisses above the line above it—"All moorhens have large green feet" and "Magnus is a moorhen". Remember that some arguments have more than one conclusion:

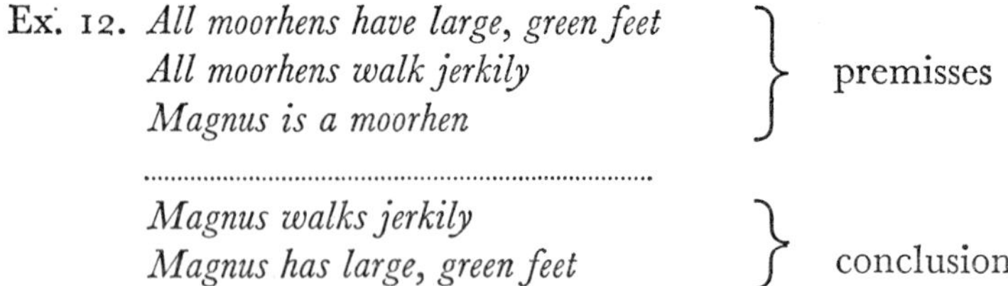

Ex. 12. All moorhens have large, green feet
All moorhens walk jerkily
Magnus is a moorhen
premisses
Magnus walks jerkily
Magnus has large, green feet
conclusions

Ex. 12 above is all right, but Ex. 11 would have to be written out as two separate arguments, with "Magnus has large green feet" appearing twice:

All moorhens have large, green feet
Magnus is a moorhen

....

Magnus has large, green feet

Magnus has large, green feet
Magnus is a bird

....

At least one bird has large, green feet.

Exercises on part II, "What is deduction?" (Answers on page 25)

(1) Which of the following arguments have the same logical form as each other?

A: If John had known that Mabel was going to the party, he would have refused the invitation. He didn't refuse the invitation: so he can't have known.

B: If he goes, I go: he's going: so I am too.

C: The deal was, if either party breaks the contract then the whole agreement is void. They've gone on strike, in other words, they've broken the contract; so we can treat the agreement as void.

D: If they suspected anything, we'd have been followed; we haven't been followed; so they don't suspect.

(2) Which of the following statements is true?

E: You can't tell if an argument is logically valid unless you know the facts of the matter it's concerned with.

F: You can tell if an argument is logically valid even if you don't know the facts.

G: You can see the logical form of an argument even if you don't know what it's all about.

H: The logical form of an argument depends on the meanings of *all* the words in it.

Exercises on part II "Statements" and "Arguments". (Answers on page 25).

(1) Underline the statements in the two following passages:

(a) We communists have been reproached with the desire of abolishing the right of personally acquiring property as the fruit of man's own labour, which property is alleged to be the groundwork of all personal freedom, activity, and independence.

Hard-won, self-acquired, self-earned property! Do you mean the property of the petty artisan and of the small peasant, a form of property that preceded the bourgeois form? There is no need to abolish that; the development of industry has to a great extent already destroyed it, and is still destroying it daily.

Or do you mean modern bourgeois private property?

But does wage labour create any property for the labourer? Not a bit. The average price of wage labour is the minimum wage. What, therefore, the wage labourer appropriates by means of his labour merely suffices to prolong and reproduce a bare existence. We by no means intend to abolish this personal appropriation of the products of labour, an appropriation that is made for the maintenance and reproduction of human life, and that leaves no surplus wherewith to command the labour of others.

(Marx & Engels, Manifesto of the Communist Party, 1888)

(b) Let me illustrate in this way. Supposing I commit a crime. As the burglar said when they brought his previous convictions against him, "It's a thing that might happen to any man." Well, now, what would happen? I belong to a body called the Authors of England. I am one of the playwrights, journalists, authors. My trade organization is the Society of Authors, Playwrights and Composers. The day after I commit the crime you would see all about it in the papers. "Bernard Shaw in the Dock", "Bernard Shaw accused of Murder", or burglary, or whatever it might be. If it was a more trivial crime the papers might say "G.B.S."

But mark this. The headline in the papers would not be "The Authors and the Public". They would not say the authors committed a murder, or committed a burglary. Agitators would not form vigilance societies to protect themselves against the authors of England. No one would suggest that I had carefully pre-arranged the crime with Mr. Galsworthy or Mr. Moore or Miss Ethel M. Dell. The responsibility would lie with me alone.

But supposing a police constable or a Chief Constable makes any mistake. What do you see next day in the paper? The mistake, or the crime, or whatever it may be, is always stated as having been committed by the police. It is always the "Police and the Public".

(George Bernard Shaw, "Censorship as a Police Duty", 1928)

(2) The following statements are the jumbled premisses and conclusions of two arguments, each of three statements. Sort the statements out into premisses and conclusions, and write the argument out as decribed on pages 21–22.

(a) All the animals in this house are cats.
(b) All cats prowl at night.
(c) All animals that prowl at night, love to gaze at the moon.
(d) All the animals in this house prowl at night.
(e) All the animals in this house love to gaze at the moon.

Answers to Exercises on part II, "What is deduction?"

(1) A & D have the same logical form, B & C have the same logical form.

(2) E, false; F, true; G, true; H, false.

If you got (1) wrong, re-read pages 13–16
If you got (2) wrong, re-read pages 13–16

Answers to exercises on part II, "Statements" and "Arguments".

(1) (a) *We communists have been reproached with the desire of abolishing the right of personally acquiring property as the fruit of man's own labour, which property is alleged to be the groundwork of all personal freedom, activity, and independence.*

Hard-won, self-acquired, self-earned property! Do you mean the property of the petty artisan and of the small peasant, a form of property that preceded the bourgeois form? *There is no need to abolish that; the development of industry has to a great extent already destroyed it, and is still destroying it daily.*

Or do you mean modern bourgeois private property?

But does wage labour create any property for the labourer? *Not a bit. The average price of wage labour is the minimum wage. What, therefore, the wage labourer appropriates by means of his labour merely suffices to prolong and reproduce a bare existence. We by no means intend to abolish this personal appropriation of the products of labour, an appropriation that is made for the maintenance and reproduction of human life, and that leaves no surplus wherewith to command the labour of others.*

(b) Let me illustrate in this way. Supposing I commit a crime. As the burglar said when they brought his previous convictions against him, ["*It's a thing that might happen to any man.*"] Well, now, what would happen? *I belong to a body called the Authors of England. I am one of the playwrights, journalists, authors. My trade organization is the Society of Authors, Playwrights and Composers. The day after I commit the crime you would see all about it in the Papers.* ["*Bernard Shaw in the Dock,*" "*Bernard Shaw accused of Murder,*" *or Burglary, or whatever it might be.*] *If it was a more trivial crime the papers might say "G.B.S."*

But mark this. *The headline in the papers would not be "The Authors and the Public". They would not say the authors committed a murder, or committed a burglary. Agitators would not form vigilance societies to protect themselves against the authors of England. No one would suggest that I had carefully pre-arranged the crime with Mr. Galsworthy or Mr. Moore or Miss Ethel M. Dell. The responsibility would lie with me alone.*

But supposing a police constable or a Chief Constable makes any mistake. What do you see next day in the paper? *The mistake, or the crime, or whatever it may be, is always stated as having been committed by the police.* [*It is always the "Police and the Public"*.]

Statements in italics. There is room for dispute over whether the sentences in square brackets are statements or not. You may with profit reflect on why this is so.

(2) *All the animals in this house are cats*
All cats prowl at night

....

All the animals in this house prowl at night

All the animals in this house prowl at night
All animals that prowl at night love to gaze at the moon

....

All animals in this house love to gaze at the moon.

(As long as you have the right pair of premisses attached to the right conclusion, it doesn't matter what order the premisses or the arguments are in.)

Part III

III Truth and Validity

Part III

III Truth and Validity

1 In this section we shall explain the difference between arguments which are logically sound and arguments which are logically unsound, and discuss whether logically sound arguments always lead us to the truth.

Arguments consist of premisses and conclusions. A logically sound argument is one in which the conclusion really does follow from the premisses. Such an argument is called **valid.**

Valid

The argument

Ex. 13. *All metals are soft*
Steel is a metal

....

Steel is soft

is a *valid* argument: the conclusion "Steel is soft" really does follow from the premisses "All metals are soft" and "Steel is a metal". The logical form of Ex. 13 is

All A are B
x is (an) A

....

x is (a) B

Validity depends on logical form. So any argument of the form

All A are B
x is A

....

x is B

will be valid, no matter what is substituted for A, B or x.

An argument in which the conclusion does *not* follow from the premisses is **invalid.** The argument

Invalid

Ex. 14. *Steel is a metal*
Steel is a conductor

....

All metals are conductors

is *invalid:* the conclusion "All metals are conductors" does not follow from the premisses "Steel is a metal" and "Steel is a conductor".

It is very important to see that a *logically sound* or *valid* argument is not necessarily one with a true conclusion, or true premisses. This is because validity and invalidity depend just on the *logical form* of the argument, which is not affected by what is substituted for A, B and x. But the *truth* of the statements involved obviously *is* affected by what you substitute for A, B and x.

Ex. 13 has one true premiss:

Steel is a metal

and one false one:

All metals are soft

Its conclusion:

Steel is soft

is also false. Nevertheless it is a *valid* argument—because validity depends on logical form, not on the truth or falsity of the conclusion.

Suppose, however, we substitute "conductor" for "soft", obtaining

Ex. 15. *All metals are conductors*
Steel is a metal
....
Steel is a conductor

Ex. 15 has the same logical form as Ex. 13; it too has the form

All A are B
x is A
....
x is B

So Ex. 15, like Ex. 13, is valid. But the statements of Ex. 15, unlike the statements of Ex. 13, are all true: by making suitable substitutions for A, B and x we have produced three true statements instead of the one true and two false statements of Ex. 13. In Ex. 14, on the other hand, we have an example of an argument whose premisses and conclusions are both true, but nevertheless the argument is invalid; its logic is faulty.

Is the following statement true or false?

All bachelors are homicidal maniacs.

---

2 Is the following statement true or false? False

All homicidal maniacs have seen the Loch Ness Monster.

---

3 Is the following statement true or false? **False**

All bachelors have seen the Loch Ness Monster

---

4 Is the following argument valid or invalid? **False**

Ex. 16. *All bachelors are homicidal maniacs*
All homicidal maniacs have seen the Loch Ness Monster
....
All bachelors have seen the Loch Ness Monster

---

5 Is the statement below true or false? **Valid**

All cats are felines

---

6 Is the statement below true or false? **True**

All animals are felines

---

7 Is the statement below true or false? **False**

All cats are animals

---

8 Is the argument **True**

Ex. 17. *All cats are felines*
All animals are felines
....
All cats are animals

valid or invalid?

---

9 An invalid argument may have true and false premisses and conclusions in any combination: true premisses and false conclusions, false premisses and true conclusions, mixed true and false premisses and mixed true and false conclusions, etc.... (there are nine possible combinations). **Invalid**

So knowing that an argument is invalid tells you *nothing* about the truth or falsity of its premisses and conclusions. However, things are slightly better with valid arguments. A valid argument can have true and false premisses and conclusions in *any combination but one:* the one exception is the combination of true premisses with a false conclusion. No valid argument can have true premisses with a false conclusion. This is one way of defining a valid argument, and explaining what we mean by saying a conclusion really does follow from its premisses: if an argument is valid (if its conclusion follows from its premisses), the truth of the premisses *guarantees* the truth of the conclusion. If the premisses are true, then the conclusion must also be true.

The next example has been deliberately chosen because you are unlikely to know the meaning of the words involved. This means you have to take on trust what I tell you about the truth or falsity of the statements involved; but nevertheless, you should be able to answer all the questions I ask about it.

The following statements are true:

All serial relations are transitive, aliorelative and connected.
The relation "greater than" is a serial relation.

Is the following argument valid or invalid?

Ex. 18. *All serial relations are transitive, aliorelative and connected.*
The relation "greater than" is a serial relation.

....

The relation "greater than" is transitive, aliorelative and connected.

---

10 Is the statement Valid

The relation "greater than" is transitive, aliorelative and connected

true or false?

---

11 Suppose you knew that the relation "greater than" was not a serial relation. Would you still be able to tell, *just from the argument* Ex. 18 above, whether or not the relation "greater than" was transitive, aliorelative and connected? True

---

12 It is important to remember the relationship between truth and validity when you evaluate real arguments in ordinary language. When you look at real arguments, you will almost certainly be chiefly interested in whether something is true or not; and you must remember that logic cannot help you very much with that. Someone who is seriously putting forward an argument, as opposed to just citing it as an example, is asserting that its conclusion is true; but all that logic can tell you is whether or not his conclusion follows from his premisses. If you want to show that his conclusion is false, it is no good just proving his argument invalid. All you accomplish by doing that, is show that your opponent has not produced a good reason for believing his conclusion to be true—but it still could be true, nevertheless. Another disadvantage of proving an argument invalid is that invalid arguments can usually be made valid easily enough by just adding or substituting an extra premiss; for example, Ex. 17 on page 31, No

All cats are felines
All animals are felines

....

All cats are animals

is invalid, but can be made valid just by adding the premiss "All felines are animals". So if it is the *truth* of a conclusion you are interested in, rather than what it follows from, proving invalidity is very inconclusive. Still, mistakes in logic are always worth pointing out! If, on the other hand, someone's argument is valid, and you want to avoid accepting his conclusions, you *must* show that at least one of his premisses is false: for if they are true, and his argument is valid, you cannot rationally avoid accepting his conclusion as true.

(1) Here is a list of statement forms:

All A are B
All A are C
All B are C
All C are B
x is a B
x is a C

Choose any three of the statement forms in the above list and use them

(a) to construct a valid argument form.
(b) Now see how many different valid argument forms you can construct of three statement forms each from the list. You should be able to get at least three.
(c) Now choose any three of the statement forms in the above list and use them to construct an invalid argument form.
(d) See how many different invalid argument forms you can get in the same way.

(2) Here are two argument forms. One is valid, one invalid

All A are B	All A are C
All B are C	All B are C
....	....
All A are C	All A are B

Here are four terms you can substitute for A, B and C in the argument forms given: crocodiles, politicians, mortals, reptiles.

Substitute one of the four terms for each of the letters in the valid argument form so that you get

(a) a valid argument with false premisses and conclusion
(b) a valid argument with true premisses and conclusion
(c) a valid argument with false premisses and a true conclusion
(d) a valid argument with one true premiss, one false premiss and a true conclusion
(e) a valid argument with one true premiss, one false premiss, and a false conclusion.
(f) Could you substitute in such a way as to get a valid argument with true premisses and a false conclusion?

Substitute one of the four terms for each of the letters in the invalid argument form so that you get

(g) an invalid argument with true premisses and a false conclusion
(h) an invalid argument with one true premiss, one false premiss, and a true conclusion
(i) an invalid argument with one true premiss, one false premiss and a false conclusion
(j) an invalid argument with true premisses and conclusion.
(k) Could you substitute in such a way as to produce an invalid argument with false premisses and a true conclusion?

N.B. For the purposes of this exercise, "mortals" should be taken in its literal sense of "things subject to death".

Answers to exercises on part III

(1a) & (1b) Valid:

All A are B
All B are C
....
All A are C

All A are C
All C are B
....
All A are B

All B are C
x is a B
....
x is a C

All C are B
x is a C
....
x is a B

The *order* of the two premisses in each of the four arguments is immaterial: provided you have the same pair of premisses attached to the same conclusion as in the above four arguments, your answer is correct (i.e. if you have,

All B are C
All A are B
....
All A are C

instead of

All A are B
All B are C
....
All A are C

your answer is still correct).

(1c) & (1d) All other argument forms than the ones given above are invalid.

(2a) Eight possibilities:

All mortals are politicians
All politicians are reptiles
....
All mortals are reptiles

All mortals are politicians
All politicians are crocodiles
....
All mortals are crocodiles

All mortals are reptiles
All reptiles are crocodiles
....
All mortals are crocodiles

All mortals are crocodiles
All crocodiles are politicians
....
All mortals are politicians

All mortals are reptiles
All reptiles are politicians
....
All mortals are politicians

All politicians are reptiles
All reptiles are crocodiles
....
All politicians are crocodiles

All reptiles are crocodiles
All crocodiles are politicians
....
All reptiles are politicians

All reptiles are politicians
All politicians are crocodiles
....
All reptiles are crocodiles

(2b) Only one possibility

All crocodiles are reptiles
All reptiles are mortals
....
All crocodiles are mortals

(2c) Only one possibility

All crocodiles are politicians
All politicians are reptiles
....
All crocodiles are reptiles

(2d) Six possibilities

All crocodiles are mortals
All mortals are reptiles
....
All crocodiles are reptiles

All politicians are reptiles
All reptiles are mortals
....
All politicians are mortals

All crocodiles are politicians
All politicians are mortals.
....
All crocodiles are mortals

All reptiles are crocodiles
All crocodiles are mortals
....
All reptiles are mortals

All politicians are crocodiles
All crocodiles are mortals
....
All politicians are mortals

All reptiles are politicians
All politicians are mortals
....
All reptiles are mortals

(2e) Eight possibilities

All crocodiles are mortals
All mortals are politicians
....
All crocodiles are politicians

All politicians are crocodiles
All crocodiles are reptiles
....
All politicians are reptiles

All politicians are mortals
All mortals are crocodiles
....
All politicians are crocodiles

All reptiles are mortals
All mortals are crocodiles
....
All reptiles are crocodiles

All politicians are mortals
All mortals are reptiles
....
All politicians are reptiles

All reptiles are mortals
All mortals are politicians
....
All reptiles are politicians

All crocodiles are reptiles
All reptiles are politicians
....
All crocodiles are politicians

All mortals are crocodiles
All crocodiles are reptiles
....
All mortals are reptiles

(2f) No: if you got this wrong, re-read pp. 31–32.

(2g) Five possibilities

All politicians are mortals
All crocodiles are mortals
....
All politicians are crocodiles

All reptiles are mortals
All crocodiles are mortals
....
All reptiles are crocodiles

All politicians are mortals
All reptiles are mortals
....
All politicians are reptiles

All reptiles are mortals
All politicians are mortals
....
All reptiles are politicians

All crocodiles are mortals
All politicians are mortals
....
All crocodiles are politicians

(2h) One possibility

All crocodiles are reptiles
All mortals are reptiles
....
All crocodiles are mortals

(2i) Three possibilities

All crocodiles are reptiles
All politicians are reptiles
....
All crocodiles are politicians

All politicians are reptiles
All crocodiles are reptiles
....
All politicians are crocodiles

All mortals are reptiles
All crocodiles are reptiles
....
All mortals are crocodiles

(2j) One possibility

All crocodiles are mortals
All reptiles are mortals
....
All crocodiles are reptiles

(2k) Yes: if you got this wrong, re-read pp. 31–32.

Part IV

IV Sentential Logic

Part IV

IV Sentential Logic

Sentences and Operators

1 In exercise 1 at the end of part III you were given a list of statement forms and asked to use them to construct an argument form. One of the argument forms you could have produced looked like this:

Ex. 19. *All A are B*
All B are C
....
All A are C

In part II we analysed an argument in words down to its basic argument form, which looked like this:

Ex. 20. *If p then q*
Not q
....
Not p

In both these argument forms, everything except the logical words has been replaced by the single letters A, B, C or p, q. So which are the logical words in Ex. 19?

---

2 Which are the logical words in Ex. 20? **All, are**

---

3 There is an important difference between the logical words of Ex. 19 and the logical words of Ex. 20. The best way of getting at it is to think back to the arguments which the two argument forms represent; i.e. to think back to what A, B and C stand for, and what p and q stand for. **If, then, not**

In exercise 2 at the end of part III you were given a list of words you could substitute for A, B and C in:

All A are B
All B are C
....
All A are C

The list was crocodiles, mortals, politicians, reptiles.

Is any of the items on this list a complete sentence?

Yes/No

---

4 In fact we cannot substitute complete sentences for A, B and C in Ex. 19 and still make sense. If you don't believe me, try it! In part II the argument form — No

If p then q
not q

....

not p

was obtained by substituting p and q for parts of the following argument:

If Stalin was a Communist then I am a Dutchman
It is not the case that I am a Dutchman

....

It is not the case that Stalin was a Communist.

Are the parts of the argument that p and q stand for complete sentences?

Yes/No

---

5 In fact, we *have* to substitute complete sentences for p and q in Ex. 20. You may remember that we tried to substitute other things than complete sentences for p and q in part II and failed to make sense. Logical words can be divided into two broad categories: those that combine with or operate on complete sentences to make new sentences, such as "if . . . then . . . " and "not" and those which operate on bits of language which are not complete sentences, such as "all" and "some". — Yes

Logical words which operate on complete sentences are called **sentential operators,** and their logic is called *sentential logic* or the **sentential calculus.** The first part of this course will be devoted to study of the sentential calculus.

Sentential operator
Sentential calculus

Some sentential operators operate on only one sentence at a time. An example is "It is not the case that" or "not"

It is not the case that | Stalin was a Communist |

A sentential operator which operates on only *one* sentence at a time is called a **unary** operator. Some sentential operators need two sentences to complete their sense. An example is "and":

Unary

| The sun is up | and | the birds are singing |

"And" plus one sentence does not make sense. Neither "the sun is up and" nor "and the birds are singing" is a complete sentence. But "The sun is up and the birds are singing" is a complete sentence. Another example of a sentential operator which needs two sentences is "If . . . then . . .":

If | the candidate is a conservationist | then | I shall vote for him |

Just as in the case of "and", neither "If the candidate is a conservationist" nor "then I shall vote for him" is a complete sentence, or makes sense on its own. Though here in English we have two logical words, "if" and "then", we count the two together as one logical operator, since in combination with the two extra sentences they make only one new sentence.

If this confuses you remember that in English it is permissible to drop the "then" and just write

If [the candidate is a conservationist]—[I shall vote for him]

A sentential operator which operates on *two* sentences at a time is called a **binary** operator.

Binary

The sentential calculus deals with arguments which use sentential operators. As the name "calculus" implies, it gives definite rules for *calculating* whether an argument using sentential operators is valid or not. There are four operators in the sentential calculus which correspond roughly to the English words "not", "and", "or" and "if . . . then . . .". These operators are to be our first subject of study.

It is important to remember that their meanings correspond only *roughly* to the meanings of "and", "not", "or" and "if . . . then": the use of the operators is much more restricted than the use of these words in ordinary English, where they are sometimes used as sentential operators, sometimes not. It will therefore be convenient to represent the operators by special signs, instead of using the English words with which they must not be confused.

We will examine each operator, and the symbol for it, in turn.

"Not"

The symbol for the sentential operator "not" is ~ (spoken "tilde", to rhyme with "Hilda")

~ *p*

means

not p

~ *Stalin was a Communist*

means *Stalin was not a Communist*

or

It is not the case that Stalin was a Communist.

What does

~ *The birds are singing*

mean?

---

6 What does

~ *George has gone to the party*

mean?

The birds are not singing
or
It is not the case that the birds are singing

---

7 What does

∼ *I like George*

mean?

George has not gone to the party
or
It is not the case that George has gone to the party.

---

8 A sentence of the form

$\sim p$

is called a **negation**

Let us now try to define *exactly* what the sentential operator does to a statement. Consider the statement

The sun is up.

Suppose that it is true—i.e. suppose that the sun really is up. In that case, is the following statement true or false?

∼ *The sun is up.*

I don't like George
or
It is not the case that I like George

Negation

---

9 Now suppose that it is *false* that the sun is up, i.e. suppose that in fact the sun is *not* up. In that case, is the following statement true or false?

∼ *The sun is up.*

False

---

10 So the effect of operating on a *true* sentence with ∼, is to produce a new sentence which is *false*, and the effect of operating on a *false* sentence with ∼, is to produce a new sentence which is *true*. We call the truth or falsity of a sentence, its **truth value.**

We can indicate the truth-value of the sentence on which the ∼ operates in the following way: when the ∼ is operating on a *true* sentence, we write

∼ T

and when ∼ is operating on a *false* sentence, we write

∼ F

In the particular logical system we are studying, it is assumed that every statement must be either true or false: there is no third possibility. It is however an open question whether every statement of ordinary language *must*, in fact, be regarded as true or false. Let us consider some examples.

A prominent politician recently opened a section of his speech with the statement, "Those whom the gods wish to destroy, they first make mad." If one were trying to analyse his speech according to the logic of the sentential calculus, one would be hard put to it to decide if this statement should be counted as true or false: this kind of distinction hardly seems relevant to such expressions. Yet the speaker presumably meant *something* by what he said.

True

Truth value

Here is a famous example from Bertrand Russell: Consider the statement

The King of France is bald

There is no king of France. So should one count this statement as true or false? Again, though for a different reason, one would be hard put to it to decide. (Russell himself decided to count it as false. But not all philosophers agree with him.)

Now consider ordinary future-tense statements, such as

England will be governed by a military dictatorship in 1984

Unless one is a believer in thorough-going determinism, one may well doubt that such a statement is true *at the time of its utterance*, if it is uttered *before* 1984—say, in 1971. For the state of affairs which is required for its truth—i.e., England's being governed by a military dictatorship in 1984—is not yet actually the case, *in 1971*: one might feel that

England will be governed by a military dictatorship in 1984

does not *become* true or false till 1984. In 1971 one cannot count it as either.

In view of these difficulties, some people think that the standard two-valued logic, with "true" and "false" as the only two possible values, is far too limited and artificial to do justice to all the possibilities. Some logicians have constructed three- or even multi-valued logical systems to try to take care of this. But the more complicated a system is, the harder it is to understand. In this course we shall be sticking to the standard, simple, two-valued sentential calculus: on the grounds that it's better to learn to walk before trying to run. If you find this irksome, remember that the charge against two-valued logic is not that it is *wrong*, but that it is *inadequate:* though most agree that in fact all statements in ordinary language need *not* be true or false, no one denies that there are some arguments which standard two-valued logic covers perfectly adequately.

Let us now return to ~.

The operator ~ *reverses* the truth value of a sentence: if "p" is true, then "~ p" is false, and if "p" is false, then "~ p" is true.

We can summarize this in a table

a	~ T = F
b	~ F = T

In the left-hand side of each row of the table we have the sentence-form containing ~, with T or F to indicate whether the sentence to which the ~ is applied is true or false; in the right-hand side we indicate the resulting truth-value for the whole negation (i.e. the sentence-form containing the ~.) The letters a, b to the left of the table are simply ways of indicating particular rows: thus by "row a" of this table, I mean the top row, i.e.,

~ T = F

and by "row b" I mean the second row, i.e.

$\sim F = T$

We can say that this table *defines the meaning* of the operator $\sim$. For all that $\sim$ does to a sentence, is that it affects its truth-value in some way; and what we have here is a table which gives all the different possible truth-values for a sentence containing $\sim$, according to the different possible truth-values of the sentence on which it operates. Such a table is called a **truth-table** for that sentence.

Truth-table

"And"

The symbol for the sentential operator "and" is & (spoken "ampersand"). "p & q" means "p and q". "The sun is up & the birds are singing" means "The sun is up and the birds are singing." What does

John plays cricket & John plays football

mean?

John plays cricket and John plays football
or
John plays cricket and football

11 A sentence of the form

p & *q*

is called a **conjunction.** The sentences linked together by the operator & (in this case "p" and "q") are called the **conjuncts** of the conjunction.

Conjunction
Conjunct

& is a *binary* sentential operator—it requires *two* sentences to complete its meaning. Consider the two sentences

Ex. 21. *The sun is up.*
Ex. 22. *The birds are singing.*

Suppose that Ex. 21 is true and Ex. 22 is false—i.e. suppose it is true that the sun is up, and false that the birds are singing. Then is the following sentence true or false?

The sun is up & the birds are singing.

---

12 Now suppose Ex. 21 is false and Ex. 22 is true—i.e. suppose it is false that the sun is up, and it is true that the birds are singing. Then is the following sentence true or false?

False

The sun is up & the birds are singing.

---

13 Now suppose Ex. 21 and Ex. 22 are both false. Then is the following sentence true or false?

False

The sun is up & the birds are singing.

---

14 Now suppose Ex. 21 and Ex. 22 are both true. Then is the following sentence true or false?

False

The sun is up & the birds are singing.

---

15 So we can see that the effect of operating on a pair of sentences with & is to produce a new sentence, a conjunction, which is true only if *both of the two original sentences, its conjuncts, are true.* If "p" and "q" are *both* true, then "p & q" is true; but if either "p" or "q", or both, are false, then "p & q" is false. We can summarize these results in a table, as before: True

a	T & T = T
b	T & F = F
c	F & T = F
d	F & F = F

This table gives all the different possible combinations of true and false sentences in a conjunction.

"Or"

Consider the following statement

Ex. 23a. *Either John's not as bright as we thought, or he hasn't been working.*

Suppose we discovered that John wasn't bright at all, and moreover hadn't been working either. Would we regard Ex. 23a as false?

Yes/No

---

16 So Ex. 23a allows for the possibility that John might be *both* not bright *and* not working. No

Now consider the following statement:

Ex. 23b. *The winner will get £1000 in cash or a holiday for two in Bermuda.*

Does this statement allow for the possibility that the winner might get *both* the cash *and* the holiday?

Yes/No

---

17 Clearly, we use the word "or" in two different senses. In one sense No

p or q

means

p or q or both

In the other sense,

p or q

means

p or q but not both

The sense of "or" which means "p or q or both" is called the **inclusive "or".** The sense of "or" which means "p or q but not both" is called the **exclusive "or".**

Inclusive "or"
Exclusive "or"

The "or" we are concerned with in the sentential calculus is the *inclusive* "or"—the sense of "or" which means "p or q or both".

The symbol for the inclusive "or" is v (spoken "vel"). So what does "p v q" mean?

---

p or q or both

18 What does

This evening I shall do my logic assignment v *I shall read the evening paper*

mean?

This evening I shall do my logic assignment or read the evening paper or both.

19 A sentence of the form

p v *q*

is called a **disjunction.** The two sentences linked by the operator v (in this case "p" and "q") are called the **disjuncts** of the disjunction. v, like &, is a binary operator—it requires two sentences to complete its meaning. Consider the two sentences:

Disjunction
Disjunct

Ex. 24. *John is innocent*
Ex. 25. *Mary is lying*

Suppose Ex. 24 is true and Ex. 25 is false. Then is the following sentence true or false?

John is innocent v *Mary is lying.*

True

20 Now suppose Ex. 24 is false and Ex. 25 is true. Then is the following sentence true or false?

John is innocent v *Mary is lying.*

True

21 Now suppose both Ex. 24 and Ex. 25 are true. Then is the following sentence true or false?

John is innocent v *Mary is lying.*

True

22 Now suppose Ex. 24 and Ex. 25 are both false. Then is the following sentence true or false?

John is innocent v *Mary is lying.*

---

23 So the effect of operating on a pair of sentences with v is to produce a new sentence, a disjunction, which is false only if both of the original sentences, its disjuncts, are false. So the table for v would look like this:

False

a	T v T = T
b	T v F = T
c	F v T = T
d	F v F = F

We can now see that what these three sentential operators do is form new sentences whose truth-value is determined by the truth-values of the sentences to which the operators are applied. If "p" is true, then "~ p" is false; if "p" is false, then "~ p" is true. If both "p" and "q" are true, then "p & q" is true; if either or both of "p" and "q" are false, then "p & q" is false. If either or both of "p" and "q" are true, then "p v q" is true; if both "p" and "q" are false, then "p v q" is false. Notice that we need not know anything about the sentences "p" and "q", other than their truth or falsity, in order to decide if sentences formed out of them with ~, & and v are true or false. Thus, for example, if we already know that the sun is up, and that the birds are not singing, we can easily determine the truth or falsity of all these sentences:

Ex. 26. ~ *The sun is up.*
Ex. 27. ~ *The birds are singing.*
Ex. 28. *The sun is up & the birds are singing.*
Ex. 29. *The sun is up* v *the birds are singing.*

Can you now say which of the above four sentences are true and which false, making the given assumption? (I.e. assuming that "The sun is up" is true, and "The birds are singing" is false.)

---

24 Because the truth-value of sentences containing the operators ~, & and v is determined solely by the truth-values of the sentences to which ~, & and v are applied, these operators are called **truth-functional operators,** and the sentences containing them are sometimes called **truth-functions** of the sentences to which the operators are applied. A truth-function is a sentence satisfying the following conditions:

Ex. 26 false Ex. 27 true
Ex. 28 false Ex. 29 true

Truth-functional operator
Truth-function

(a) It is formed by applying a sentential operator to some other sentence(s).
(b) Its truth-value is determined solely by the truth-values of its constituent sentence(s).

Exercise on part IV

Given that the following statements are true:

John is innocent
The crime was committed before midnight
The murderer is a member of the household
The police inspector is baffled

and given that the following statements are false:

Mary is lying
The victim suspected nothing
John has an alibi

which of the following statements are true, and which are false?

1. John is innocent & Mary is lying.
2. The victim suspected nothing v the crime was committed before midnight.
3. ~ Mary is lying.
4. The victim suspected nothing & John has an alibi.
5. The crime was committed before midnight v the murderer is a member of the household.
6. ~ the murderer is a member of the household.
7. Mary is lying v John has an alibi.
8. John is innocent & the police inspector is baffled.

Answers to Exercise on part IV

True: 2, 3, 5, 8
False: 1, 4, 6, 7

Part V

V The Operator →

V The Operator →

1 We can now discuss the last of the four logical operators of the sentential calculus, "if . . . then . . .". The symbol for "if . . . then . . ." is → (spoken "arrow"). We translate "p → q" as "if p, then q". How would we translate the following sentence?

John is innocent → Mary is lying.

---

2 How would we translate the following sentence?

Mary is lying → John is innocent.

If John is innocent, then Mary is lying

---

3 It is important to remember that the statement to the *left* of the arrow *always* represents the statement after the "if", and the statement to the *right* of the arrow *always* represents the statement after the "then". Sometimes in English the order of an "if . . . then . . ." statement is reversed; instead of

If John has told the police, then Mary is in danger

we say

Mary is in danger if John has told the police.

Both of these two sentences would be translated by

John has told the police → Mary is in danger.

A sentence of the form

$p \rightarrow q$

is called a **conditional.** The sentence to the *left* of the arrow, the sentence after the "if" (in this case "p") is called the **antecedent** of the conditional. The sentence to the *right* of the arrow, or the sentence after the "then" (in this case "q") is called the **consequent** of the conditional.

What is the antecedent of the following conditional?

John is innocent → Mary is lying.

If Mary is lying, then John is innocent

Conditional

Antecedent

Consequent

---

4 What is the consequent of the following conditional?

Mary is lying → John is innocent.

John is innocent

---

5 What is the antecedent of the following conditional?

If you have finished, then you can go.

John is innocent

---

6 What is the consequent of the following conditional?

You can go if you've finished.

You have finished

The meaning of $\rightarrow$.

You can go

7 What is difficult about $\rightarrow$ is understanding the relationship of $\rightarrow$ to the English expression "if . . . then . . .". For though we usually translate $\rightarrow$ with "if . . . then . . .", in fact there is *no* English expression which exactly captures the meaning of $\rightarrow$. The vital thing to remember is that $\rightarrow$, like $\sim$, & and v, is a *truth-functional operator:* when applied to sentences it forms new sentences whose truth-value depends solely on the truth-value of the sentences to which it is applied. In other words, the truth or falsity of

$p \rightarrow q$

depends *entirely* on the truth or falsity of "p" and "q"; the meaning of $\rightarrow$ is defined by a truth-table, as follows:

a	T $\rightarrow$ T = T
b	T $\rightarrow$ F = F
c	F $\rightarrow$ T = T
d	F $\rightarrow$ F = T

The deficiencies of the "if . . . then . . ." translation of $\rightarrow$ can be seen if we consider a few examples.

Consider the sentence

The moon is made of green cheese $\rightarrow$ sugar is sweet

Is the sentence "The moon is made of green cheese", true or false?

---

8 Is the sentence "Sugar is sweet", true or false?

False

---

9 Now look at the truth-table for $\rightarrow$, above. According to the table, is the sentence

True

The moon is made of green cheese $\rightarrow$ sugar is sweet

true or false?

---

10 But we have said that we would translate

The moon is made of green cheese → sugar is sweet
by

Ex. 30. *If the moon is made of green cheese, then sugar is sweet.*

Yet we would not normally regard Ex. 30 as true, simply on the grounds that "The moon is made of green cheese" is false, and "sugar is sweet" is true. Or, again, consider the sentence

All the Apollo Moonshots were successful → the pound sterling was not devalued between 1964 *and* 1970.

Is "All the Apollo Moonshots were successful" true or false?

True

---

11 Is "The pound sterling was not devalued between 1964 and 1970" true or false?

False:
Apollo 13 was unsuccessful

---

12 According to the table on p. 54 is

All the Apollo Moonshots were successful → the pound was not devalued between 1964 and 1970
true or false?

False:
The pound was devalued in 1967

---

13 Yet again, the usual translation of this sentence, i.e.

If all the Apollo Moonshots were successful, then the pound was not devalued between 1964 and 1970

would not normally be considered true, just on the grounds that "All the Apollo Moonshots were successful" and "the pound was not devalued between 1964 and 1970" are both *false*. And this indicates exactly what is the trouble: normally we do *not* regard the English expression "if . . . then . . ." as a truth-functional operator. We would not normally regard an "if . . . then . . ." statement as true, unless there were some sort of connection, usually a causal connection, between the two statements joined by the "if . . . then . . .". The mere truth or falsity of these is not the primary consideration. Thus, though we would not be inclined to regard

If all the Apollo Moonshots were successful, then the pound was not devalued between 1964 and 1970

as true, we would be much more inclined to regard

If all the Apollo Moonshots are successful, then the American space programme will receive more public support

as true. Moreover, we might well have good grounds for regarding it as true even if we still did not know whether or not the Apollo Moonshots were all successful, or whether or not the space programme was receiving more public support: in other words, when we were without information about the truth or falsity of the statements joined by the "if . . . then . . .". This amply demonstrates that "if . . .

True

then . . ." in at least some very common usages is definitely *not* just a truth-functional operator. Why then do we use "if . . . then . . ." as the translation of → ? Is there any real connection between the two expressions?

The answer to this question is rather complicated. First I should like to point out one fact about the ordinary usage of "if . . . then . . ." It seems absurd at first to offer → as an analysis or translation of "if . . . then . . .", since the truth-table definition of → gives such extraordinary results as

Ex. 30. *If the moon is made of green cheese then sugar is sweet.*

coming out true. But in fact we do ordinarily use "if . . . then . . ." in a sense which is not causal at all, and which requires us to accept statements just as extraordinary as Ex. 30 as true. This is the sense of "if . . . then . . . " which occurs in, for example,

If Stalin was a Communist, then I'm a Dutchman.

Clearly *this* statement is no more causal, and no less absurd, than is

If the moon is made of green cheese then sugar is sweet.

But since it occurs in the familiar context of a current idiom, where we have no expectation of finding a causal statement, it does not strike us as ridiculous in the same way as a similar statement such as Ex. 30, occurring baldly as an example without the conventional idiomatic context which would help us to assess its meaning correctly. In short, we *do* actually use and recognize a non-causal sense of "if . . . then . . ." which allows as true statements which are no less bizarre than those allowed by the truth-table for →. We would not offer

If Stalin was a Communist, then I'm a Dutchman

as the premiss of an argument (which, as I showed in part II, the idiom requires us to do) if we were not prepared to accept it as true.

This preamble is intended to convince you that you should not be too impressed by the peculiar results given by the truth-table: the peculiarity may be a rather unimportant red-herring. However, I have still said nothing to justify a truth-table analysis of "if . . . then . . .", or the particular truth-table I gave you for →.

I think the best justification of the truth-table is that it is in accord with the ways we actually argue with "if . . . then . . ."; it is not just an artificially contrived logician's fiction. This will come out if we consider a few examples. The point of these examples is to show you that though the truth-table may seem at first to give bizarre results as an analysis of "if . . . then . . .", in fact it does incorporate characteristic features of the way we use "if . . . then . . ." in arguments.

For our first example we shall go back to Ex. 1, from part II:

Ex. 1. *If Stalin was a Communist, then I'm a Dutchman*
I am not a Dutchman
....
Stalin was not a Communist.

When we first looked at the expression, "If Stalin was a Communist then I'm a Dutchman" in part II, I suggested that our idiomatic use of it as an oblique way of saying "Stalin was not a Communist" relied on our tacitly accepting as valid an argument of the form of Ex. 1. Now, as I explained in part III, to claim that an argument is valid is to claim that *if* its premisses are true, its conclusion *must* be true: and here we have the link between the way we actually argue and the truth-tables. One of the ways we argue is by accepting Ex. 1 as valid: by claiming that *if* its premisses are true, its conclusion *must* be true. So let us assume that the two premisses of Ex. 1 are true, and then see if, given this one assumption, we can discover if according to the truth-tables its conclusion *must* be true.

The premisses of Ex. 1 are

Stalin was a Communist → *I'm a Dutchman*

∼ *I am a Dutchman.*

We are assuming that both these premisses are true. We want to see what the truth-tables tell us, given this assumption. Let us take first the *second* premiss, i.e.:

∼ *I am a Dutchman*

Here is the truth-table for ∼ again:

a	∼T = F
b	∼F = T

This table gives us the truth-values for the two different forms of negation that are possible. What are these two negations? (Just quote the relevant column of the truth-table.)

---

14 According to the truth-table, only *one* of these is true. Which?

∼T
∼F

---

15 So if we assume that

∼ *I'm a Dutchman*

is *true*, then one consequence of our assumption is that

I'm a Dutchman

must be

true/false.

∼F

---

16 Bearing this in mind, we now turn to the other premiss:

Stalin was a Communist → *I'm a Dutchman.*

We know that

False

I'm a Dutchman

is *false*; so we can represent the other premiss by

Stalin was a Communist → *F*

i.e. as a conditional with a false consequent.

Here is the truth-table for → again:

a	T → T = T
b	T → F = F
c	F → T = T
d	F → F = T

On which rows of the truth-table do you find conditionals with false consequents?

---

17 Which if any of these conditionals are true? (Write out the conditional(s), not the whole row of the truth-table).

Rows b and d

---

18 How about the antecedent of this true conditional; is it true or false?

F → F

---

19 So according to the truth-table, if

Stalin was a Communist → *F*

is *true*, then

Stalin was a Communist

must be

true/false.

False

---

20 Now, if

Stalin was a Communist

is *false*, then, according to the truth-table for ~,

~ *Stalin was a Communist*

must be

true/false.

False

---

21 But "~ Stalin was a Communist" means "Stalin was not a Communist" which is the conclusion of Ex. 1. So you can see that, if we assume that the two premisses of Ex. 1 are true, the truth-tables for

True

$\sim$ and $\rightarrow$ leave us no choice but to regard the conclusion of Ex. 1 as true also: in other words, according to the truth-tables, the argument in Ex. 1 is valid.

Let me just summarize this process. The truth functional account of this example is:

We are able to infer

$\sim p$

from the two premisses

$p \rightarrow q$

$\sim q$

because: (a) if $\sim$ q is true, q (according to the truth-table for $\sim$) is false. Hence the consequent of p $\rightarrow$ q is false; (b) if the consequent of a true conditional is false, then its antecedent must be false—for (according to the truth-table) the *only* possible true conditional with a false consequent is one with a false antecedent.

So you can see that if we *accept* a truth-functional account of the argument:

If Stalin was a Communist, then I'm a Dutchman
I'm not a Dutchman

....

Stalin was not a Communist

and then check the validity of the inference by reference to truth-tables, we end up with exactly those results which we feel instinctively to be right, when we argue informally. The truth-table account is at the very least *in accord* here with ordinary practice.

There is another very important point to make here. If you look back to part II you will find that the same analysis is offered of *four different* arguments:

Ex. 1. *If Stalin was a Communist then I'm a Dutchman.*
I am not a Dutchman.
Therefore, Stalin was not a Communist.

Ex. 2. *If Kipling was a poet, then I'm a Dutchman.*
I am not a Dutchman.
Therefore, Kipling was not a poet.

Ex. 3. *If this liquid is an acid, then it turns blue litmus paper red.*
It does not turn blue litmus paper red.
Therefore, it is not an acid.

Ex. 4. *If the note was typed on the office typewriter, then the e's in the text are smudged.*
The e's in the text are not smudged.
Therefore, the note was not typed on the office typewriter.

Notice that the "if . . . then . . ." in these four arguments is clearly *not* causal in the first two, and probably causal in the last two. But the truth-functional analysis I have just given obviously spans all four arguments: it will work for the last two no less than the first two. So though it may seem more reasonable to offer → as the translation of the "if . . . then . . ." in just the *first* two arguments, where the "if . . . then . . ." is clearly *not* causal, in fact the truth-functional explanation fits all four equally well: the *causal* nature of the "if . . . then . . ." in the last two examples does not seem to change the structure of the argument in any way.

In this example we made direct use only of the 2nd and 4th rows of the truth-table (though we "used" the other rows indirectly in accepting that all other rows were as they were, and were irrelevant here.)

We still have to account for the first and third rows of the truth-table—that is, find common forms of argument which are in accord with them.

I think you will accept that the following argument is clearly valid:

Ex. 31. *If you have swallowed arsenic, you will die.*
You have swallowed arsenic

....

You will die.

Let us see what the truth-tables have to say about its validity. As before, we assume that the two premisses of Ex. 31 are true, and see if according to the truth-tables the truth of the premisses is sufficient to guarantee the truth of the conclusion.

We assume that both the premisses of Ex. 31 are true. One of these premisses is "You have swallowed arsenic". If we assume that this premiss is true, which of the following representations of the other premiss, "If you have swallowed arsenic you will die" is correct?

You have swallowed arsenic → T
T → you will die
You have swallowed arsenic → F
F → you will die.

---

22 So the first premiss of Ex. 31 is conditional with a true antecedent/consequent

T → you will die

---

23 Now look at the truth-table for → again:

Antecedent

a	T → T = T
b	T → F = F
c	F → T = T
d	F → F = T

Write out the two rows of the table which refer to conditionals with true antecedents:

$T \rightarrow T = T$
$T \rightarrow F = F$

24 Is our premiss

T → *you will die*

assumed to be true or false? (You don't need to look at the truth-table for this one!)

True: we are assuming it to be true, to test the validity of the argument.

25 According to the truth-table, which of

$T \rightarrow T$
$T \rightarrow F$

is true?

$T \rightarrow T$

26 So should our premiss

T → *you will die*

be represented by

$T \rightarrow T$

or by

$T \rightarrow F$?

$T \rightarrow T$

27 So is

you will die

true or false?

True

28 "You will die" is the conclusion of Ex. 31. Thus, once again, the truth-tables show that if we assume the truth of the premisses of Ex. 31, we are bound to accept that the conclusion of Ex. 31 must also be true. In other words, the truth-tables show that Ex. 31 is valid. So we find, once more, that the truth-table gives the results which accord with ordinary practice. This time we used directly rows a and b of the table: so now we only have row c unaccounted for. This time we will consider not a valid but an *invalid* argument. Consider the following argument:

Ex. 32. *If Carstairs has been elected Treasurer, the Society will get into debt next year.*
The Society will get into debt next year.
....
Carstairs has been elected Treasurer.

It may surprise you to learn that Ex. 32 is in fact *invalid*. The reason is simple: though the first premiss states that if Carstairs has been elected Treasurer, the Society will get into debt next year (i.e. that Carstairs' being elected Treasurer would be *one* way for the Society to get into debt) it does *not* state that this is the *only* way that the Society could get into debt next year: it might be perfectly true that if Carstairs were elected Treasurer, the Society would get into debt, and yet the Society might get into debt without Carstairs being elected Treasurer at all. Whoever was elected instead might turn out to be just as incompetent as Carstairs. For this reason it would not be safer to infer

Carstairs has been elected Treasurer

just from the two premisses

If Carstairs has been elected Treasurer, the Society will get into debt next year

and

The Society will get into debt next year.

Ex. 32 too is covered by the truth-table for →. This time our two premisses are of the form "p → q" and "q". Since "q" is true (= is a premiss), the conditional which is our other premiss (= is true) can be represented

$p \rightarrow T$

to show that it has a true consequent.

Here is the truth-table for → again:

a	T → T = T
b	T → F = F
c	F → T = T
d	F → F = T

Which rows of the truth-table refer to conditionals with true consequents?

---

29 What are the conditionals on these two rows?

Rows a and c

---

30 Is either, both or neither of these conditionals true?

T → T
F → T

---

31 What about the antecedents of the two conditionals: are they true or false?

Both are true

---

32 So from the truth of a conditional and the truth of its consequent, what can one infer about the truth or falsity of its antecedent?

One is true, one false

---

33 So here again we see the truth-table giving results in accord with ordinary practice.

Nothing: any conditional with a true consequent is true, regardless of the truth or falsity of its antecedent

We have now found cases of ordinary intuitive arguing which seem to justify all four rows of the truth-table for →. I hope that as a result of this, you will agree with me that though the truth-table account of "if . . . then . . ." may at first seem artificial, it is in fact perfectly in accord with the ways in which we actually argue—which do not seem artificial at all. Moreover, arguments based on the truth-table for $\rightarrow$ may be applied to *all* the different usages of "if . . . then . . ." including the causal usage; though arguments based on causal senses of "if . . . then . . ." are not in general applicable to the truth-functional sense of "if . . . then . . .".

So one of the advantages of accepting the truth-table definition of $\rightarrow$ as an analysis of "if . . . then . . ." is that it provides us with a systematic, economical and convenient "explanation" (or, if you prefer, a *summary* or a *chart*) of very many common forms of argument. One must balance this advantage of the calculus against its disadvantages; which are, that the calculus is unrealistic to the extent that it requires you to count as true statements which you might not normally count as true (such statements as "If the moon is made of green cheese then sugar is sweet"); and that it does not cover, or attempt to cover, all the subtleties of meaning of "if . . . then . . .". Perhaps the simplest way to look at the relationship between $\rightarrow$ and "if . . . then . . ." is to think of "if . . . then . . ." as having a basic truth-functional core of meaning which persists through all its different senses, and to which, in some of its senses, additional layers of meaning may be added.

1. Find the Exercises on part IV. Using the same set of true and false sentences given in the Exercises on part IV, are the following sentences true or false?

(a) The victim suspected nothing → the murderer is a member of the household.
(b) John is innocent → the police inspector is baffled.
(c) The crime was committed before midnight → John has an alibi.
(d) John has an alibi → the crime was committed before midnight.
(e) The victim suspected nothing → Mary is lying.
(f) John is innocent → Mary is lying.

2. Are the following sentences true or false?

(a) Pigs can fly → all men are mortal.
(b) London is the capital of England → pigs can fly.
(c) Pigs can fly → cows can jump over the moon.
(d) 2 is the square root of 4 → 7 is an odd number.

1. True: a, b, d, e.
False: c, f.

2. True: a, c, d.
False: b.

Part VI

VI Translation ~

Part VI

VI Translation: ~

1 You should have a good grasp of the truth-table definitions of ~, &, v and →; so we can turn our attention to the business of recognizing them when they occur in ordinary language. The purpose of the next two parts is to enable you to translate readily from ordinary language into logical symbols, and from logical symbols into ordinary language. Translation is obviously very important if you want to apply the logic you learn to arguments in ordinary language; for only if you can translate correctly will you be able to apply correctly what you have learnt.

You may remember that in part IV I stressed that the words "not", "and", "or" and "if . . . then . . ." are only rough approximations to the four sentential operators. The reasons for this are two-fold. On the one hand, "not", "and", "or" and "if . . . then . . ." are used in a number of ways in ordinary language, not all of which correspond to the use in logic of a sentential operator; and on the other hand, there are many ways of expressing the four sentential operators in English, not all of which involve the use of the words "not", "and", "or" and "if . . . then . . .". You will see why this is so if you reflect for a moment on the nature of sentential operators. Sentential operators combine only with sentences; they combine only with sentences which are true or false; and the result of these combinations is a sentence whose truth or falsity depends solely on the truth or falsity of the sentences combined. *Any* expression of ordinary English which performs these functions, and performs them in a way which parallels the functioning of one or other of the four operators, will count as an occurrence of that operator. Thus you will find that many English expressions may be translated by the *same* operator, even though they differ subtly from each other in meaning. This is inevitable, for we use language for all sorts of other purposes than just to express logical operations; and when we are translating into logical symbols, all these other purposes are ignored. The word "translation" is really rather a misnomer here; for the aim of translation into logical symbols is quite different from the aims of most other kinds of translation. In the ordinary way, when we translate from one language into another, we try to get a version which corresponds as closely as possible in every detail to the original: this is our standard for a "good" translation. But the aim of translation into logical symbols is just to expose the *logic* of what is being translated; the aim of translation into the symbols of the sentential calculus is just to expose the *sentential* logic of what is being translated. Everything which does not affect this can safely be ignored, without detriment to the quality of the translation. When we translate expressions with subtly different shades of meaning by the same operator, this is because, from the point of view of the sentential calculus, their *logic* at any rate is identical, no matter how much they differ from each other in other ways. You should have no difficulties with translation if you bear these principles firmly in mind.

Let us see how these general remarks about translation apply to each of the four operators in turn.

It is important to remember that though we translate "$\sim$ p" as "not p", $\sim$ is *not* just a substitute for the word "not", but a sentential operator whose function is a negation. The nearest English equivalent is really not "not" but "it is not the case that . . . " in front of a sentence—but this is not very commonly used in English! "It is not the case that . . .", like "not" reverses the truth-value of the sentence to which it is applied. But *any* expression which does this, counts as a negation, and can be translated by $\sim$: and in English there are multifarious ways of negating statements without using the word "not" at all. One obvious example is the prefix "un-" in front of an adjective: for example

He is unknown in Latin America

which means the same as

He is not known in Latin America

which means the same as

It is not the case that he is known in Latin America

which can be translated as

$\sim$ *he is known in Latin America*

But there are other, less obvious, examples.

Consider the following expressions:

Ex. 33. *He didn't show up yesterday*
Ex. 34. *He never showed up yesterday*
Ex. 35. *He failed to show up yesterday*

All these statements can be read as negations. When we want to translate an English negation into a form using $\sim$, we look for the statement which is *denied* by the negation: the statement which must be *false* if the negation is *true*. What is the statement which must be *false*, if

Ex. 33. *He didn't show up yesterday*

is *true*?

---

2 So how would we translate

Ex. 33. *He didn't show up yesterday*

using $\sim$?

He showed up yesterday

---

3 What is the statement which must be *false*, if

Ex. 34. *He never showed up yesterday*

is *true*?

$\sim$ He showed up yesterday

---

4 So how would we translate

Ex. 34. *He never showed up yesterday*

using ∼?

He showed up yesterday

---

5 What is the statement which must be *false,* if

Ex. 35. *He failed to show up yesterday*

is *true*?

∼ He showed up yesterday

---

6 So how would we translate

Ex. 35. *He failed to show up yesterday*

using ∼?

He showed up yesterday

---

7 Thus you see that we can translate *all three* examples—Ex. 33, Ex. 34 and Ex. 35—by the same negation—

∼ *He showed up yesterday.*

This is because implicit in each of them is the negation of the *same* statement—

He showed up yesterday

and this is all we are interested in, from the point of view of the sentential calculus. All the other things that may be implicit in each of the three sentences are irrelevant.

You may not agree that our three examples in fact negate the same statement: you may have thought that the statement negated by

Ex. 34. *He never showed up yesterday*

was, say,

Ex. 34a. *He showed up at some time yesterday*

and the statement negated by

Ex. 35. *He failed to show up yesterday*

was

Ex. 35a. *He succeeded in showing up yesterday.*

It is true that a case can be made out for this view, and if you were to translate Ex. 34 as

∼ *He showed up at some time yesterday*

and

He failed to show up yesterday

as

∼ *He succeeded in showing up yesterday*

∼ He showed up yesterday

you would not necessarily be wrong. However, you would not necessarily be right, either—for there is no doubt that such expressions as

He never showed up yesterday
He failed to show up yesterday

are commonly used simply as straightforward negations of

He showed up yesterday

in no way distinguished from the ordinary negation with "not". It would depend on the context which was the most appropriate translation. Notice too that if either of Exs. 34a and 35a is true, then so is the plain

He showed up yesterday;

so whatever *else* is negated by

He never showed up yesterday
He failed to show up yesterday

certainly

He showed up yesterday

is negated by them *as well.* So

∼ *He showed up yesterday*

would always be a safe bet as a translation of either of Exs. 34 and 35 in that it would certainly never be false when the statement it was translating, was true. But if there is any point at all in making a fuss about the greater appropriateness of

∼ *He succeeded in showing up yesterday*

compared to

∼ *He showed up yesterday*

as the translation of

He failed to show up yesterday

it must be due to the possibility that one of them might be true when the other was false; if this possibility does not arise, then clearly the different nuances of translation will be irrelevant to truth-functional logic.

There are in English many expressions which serve to soften the brutality of an outright negation: we may prefer to say, for example

He's hardly the best man for the job

instead of the bald

He's not the best man for the job.

Again, in certain circumstances, we may prefer to say

It isn't as if she knew

instead of

She doesn't know.

When we use these two expressions in these senses, the two sentences

He's hardly the best man for the job
It isn't as if she knew

would be rendered

~ *He's the best man for the job*
~ *She knows.*

Notice also that the sentence which is actually being negated need not appear in the ordinary language version in the form which it takes in the version with ~; before you can produce the version with ~, some re-writing is often necessary. The sentence negated in

He failed to show up yesterday

is

He showed up yesterday

the sentence negated in

It isn't as if she knew

is

She knows.

So before we convert these two ordinary-language negations into a form using ~, the form of their verbs has to be adjusted, in order to achieve something like idiomatic English.

Which statement is being negated in the following statement?

Ex. 36. *He'll never make it to Istanbul without a spare tyre.*

---

8 Which statement is being negated in the following sentence?

Ex. 37. *I hardly think Carstairs will make a good treasurer.*

He will make it to Istanbul without a spare tyre

---

9 Which statement is being negated in the following sentence

Ex. 38. *She's not the only girl in the world.*

Carstairs will make a good Treasurer
or
I think Carstairs will make a good Treasurer

---

10 Which statement is being negated in the following sentence?

Ex. 39. *You never told me you were married.*

She is the only girl in the world

---

11 Which statement is being negated in the following sentence?

Ex. 40. *The alarm failed to go off.*

You told me you were married

---

12 Which statement is being negated in the following sentence?

Ex. 41. *I haven't a thing to wear tonight.*

The alarm went off

---

13 Re-write the negations Exs. 36–41 in a form using ~.

{I have got / I have} something to wear tonight

---

14 There are some negations which call for particular care when it comes to deciding exactly what statement is being negated. Such negations are those in which the words "some" "all" "no" or "none' appear. Consider for example the statement

All the natives are unfriendly.

On the analogy of

He is unknown in Latin America

which we translated as

~ *He is known in Latin America*

you might be tempted to translate

All the natives are unfriendly

as

~ *All the natives are friendly.*

Would this be correct?

Yes/No.

Ex. 36. ~ He will make it to Istanbul without a spare tyre.
Ex. 37. ~ (I think) Carstairs will make a good Treasurer.
Ex. 38. ~ She is the only girl in the world
Ex. 39. ~ You told me you were married
Ex. 40. ~ The alarm went off
Ex. 41. ~ {I have / I've got} something to wear tonight

---

15 Let us see why this is so.

Remember that the nearest English equivalent of ~ is "It is not the case that . . ." Using this expression, how would you translate

~ *All the natives are friendly?*

No

---

16 Does

It is not the case that all the natives are friendly

mean the same as

All the natives are unfriendly?

If you think the two sentences *do* mean the same: go to frame 17 on page 73.

If you think the two sentences *do not* mean the same: go to frame 20 on page 74.

It is not the case that all the natives are friendly

From frame 16

17 You're wrong: the two statements do *not* mean the same. Suppose a few of the natives are friendly, but most are unfriendly. Then would

All the natives are unfriendly

be true or false?

---

18 In the same circumstances—some natives friendly, some unfriendly—would

False

It is not the case that all the natives are friendly

be true or false?

---

19 So you see, since one sentence is true and the other false under the same set of circumstances, they cannot both mean the same. Now go on to frame 21 on page 75.

True

From frame 16

20 You are quite right: well done. The two sentences cannot mean the same, for if some of the natives were friendly and some weren't then "All the natives are unfriendly" would be false, and "It is not the case that all the natives are friendly" would be true. Sentences which do not have the same truth-value under the same set of circumstances cannot mean the same thing.

Carry on to frame 21 on page 75.

From frames 19 and 20

21 A more idiomatic version of the sentence

It is not the case that all the natives are friendly

would be just

Not all the natives are friendly.

So what we have just discovered is that there is a very important distinction between

All the natives are unfriendly (not-friendly)

and

Not all the natives are friendly.

We have seen that

Not all the natives are friendly

is translated by

$\sim$ *All the natives are friendly*

but how would we translate

All the natives are unfriendly

as a negation, using $\sim$?

We have discussed a situation in which a few of the natives were friendly, but most weren't. One way of describing this situation would be with the statement

Some of the natives are friendly.

So if the statement

Some of the natives are friendly

is *true,* then the statement

All the natives are unfriendly

would be

true/false?

---

22 Suppose now that

False

Some of the natives are friendly

is *false.* Then the statement

All the natives are unfriendly

would be

true/false?

---

23 Now suppose that

All the natives are unfriendly

is *true*. Then would

Some of the natives are friendly

be

true/false?

True

---

24 And if

All the natives are unfriendly

is *false*, then

Some of the natives are friendly

is

true/false?

False

---

25 So when

Some of the natives are friendly

is true, then

All the natives are unfriendly

is false, and *vice-versa;* and when

All the natives are unfriendly

is true, then

Some of the natives are friendly

is false, and *vice-versa*. In other words, the two statements *reverse each other's truth-value*. Now, remember I said at the beginning of this part that *any* expression which reversed the truth-value of a statement could count as its negation, and could be translated using ~, somehow or other. Since

Some of the natives are friendly

is true when

All the natives are unfriendly

is false, and false when it is true, the statement

Some of the natives are friendly

counts as the negation of

All the natives are unfriendly

and since

All the natives are unfriendly

True

is true when

Some of the natives are friendly

is false, and false when it is true, the statement

All the natives are unfriendly

counts as the negation of the statement

Some of the natives are friendly.

If we represent

All the natives are unfriendly

as "p", we can represent

Some of the natives are friendly

as "$\sim$ p"; and if instead we represent

Some of the natives are friendly

as "p", how could we represent

All the natives are unfriendly?

---

26 So the translation of $\sim$p

All the natives are unfriendly

as a negation using $\sim$ would be, *not*

$\sim$ *All the natives are friendly*

but

$\sim$ *Some of the natives are friendly.*

Now let us look at another example. Consider the statement

Some swans are not white.

Which of the following statements would you say it negates?

Some swans are white
All swans are white.

If you think it negates "Some swans are white": go to frame 27 on page 78.

If you think it negates "All swans are white": go to frame 37 on page 80.

From frame 26

27 You are wrong: in fact "Some swans are not white" is the negation of "All swans are white". The explanation of this example is as follows: A negation reverses the truth-value of the statement it negates—if a statement is true, its negation must be false; if a statement is false, its negation must be true. So it could *never* be the case that a statement and its negation were *either* both true at the same time, *or* both false at the same time.

Consider the two statements

Mary is a widow
Mary is not a widow.

Could they both be true at the same time?

---

28 Could they both be false at the same time? — No

---

29 Is one statement the negation of the other? — No

---

30 Now consider the two statements — Yes

Some swans are white
Some swans are not white.

Could they both be true at the same time?

---

31 Is one the negation of the other? — Yes: there can be both black swans and white swans in the world at the same time.

---

32 Now consider the two statements — No

Some swans are not white
All swans are white.

Could they both be true at the same time?

---

33 Could they both be false at the same time? — No

---

34 Is one the negation of the other? — No

---

35 Re-write

Some swans are not white

as a negation using ~. | Yes

---

36 Now go to frame 38 on page 80. | ~ All swans are white

From frame 26

37 Quite right: "Some swans are not white" is the negation of "All swans are white", for it is true when "All swans are white" is false, and false when "All swans are white" is true.

Carry on to frame 38 below.

From frames 36 and 37

38 Since a statement's negation is anything that reverses its truth-value, clearly if p is the negation of q, then q is also the negation of p.

Re-write

All swans are white

as a negation using ~.

∼ Some swans are not white

39 Let us consider another example; this time:

No swans are white.

Which of the following statements do you think it negates?

Some swans are white
No swans are not white
All swans are white.

If you think it negates "Some swans are white": go to frame 49 on page 83.

If you think it negates "No swans are not white": go to frame 40 on page 81.

If you think it negates "All swans are white": go to frame 41 on page 81.

From frame 39

40 Wrong—the correct answer is "Some swans are white". In fact, "No swans are not white" means exactly the same as "All swans are white", so you have made the same mistake as if you had picked "All swans are white".

Go to frame 41 below.

From frames 39 and 40

41 If you have picked "All swans are white", you have picked the wrong answer: the correct answer is "Some swans are white".

If "All swans are white" were negated by "No swans are white", then these two sentences could neither both be true at the same time, nor both false at the same time. But could

No swans are white
All swans are white

both be true at the same time?

---

42 Could

No swans are white
All swans are white

both be false at the same time?

No

---

43 If two statements are both false at the same time, can either sentence be a negation of the other?

Yes: if some but not all swans were white, the two statements would both be false.

---

44 So can either of "No swans are white" and "All swans are white" be a negation of the other?

No

---

45 Now consider the pair

No swans are white
Some swans are white.

Could they both be true at the same time?

No

---

46 Could they both be false at the same time? | No

47 Is one sentence of the pair the negation of the other? | No

48 Now go to frame 50 on page 83. | Yes

From frame 39

49 Well done: you are quite right, for "No swans are white", is true when "Some swans are white" is false, and false when it is true. Go on to frame 50 below.

Yes

From frames 48 and 49

50 Re-write "No swans are white" as a negation using ~.

---

51 Statements which are negations of each other, i.e. statement pairs which cannot be both false or both true at the same time, are sometimes also called **contradictories** of each other. Statements like

~ Some swans are not white

Contradictory

All swans are white
No swans are white

which cannot both be true at the same time, but can both be false at the same time, are sometimes called **contraries** of each other. Statements like

Contrary

Some swans are white
Some swans are not white

which can both be true at the same time, but nevertheless seem to state opposing things, are sometimes called **sub-contraries** of each other. It is important not to confuse the contradictory of a statement with its contrary or sub-contrary when translating with ~. A statement is correctly represented by ~ plus its contradictory. It is not correctly represented by ~ plus its contrary or sub-contrary.

Sub-contrary

Remember to watch out for these complications whenever you are dealing with sentences containing such words as "all", "some", "every", "no", "none",—remember that that includes sentences with words such as "sometimes", "always", "never". You will also occasionally find sentences which appear to be negations, but which you will not be able to express in forms using ~. An example is "Some people are never happy".

Translate the following sentences as idiomatically as you can, into forms which do not contain the symbol ~.

~ *I sometimes go to work by car.*

---

52 ~ *All politicians are arrogant.*

I never go to work by car

---

53 ~ *Any artists are gentlemen.*

Not all politicians are arrogant

---

54 Translate the following sentences into forms containing the symbol ~.

Sometimes I do not go to work by car.

No artist is a gentleman

---

55 *Politicians are never arrogant.*

~ I always go to work by car

---

56 *Some citizens are not electors.*

~ Politicians are sometimes arrogant
or
~ Politicians are arrogant

~ All citizens are electors

Exercises on part VI

Translate the following sentences into negations, using $\sim$.

1. I fail to see why the ratepayers of this Borough should finance the Council's inefficiency.
2. All politicians are unhappy.
3. He will never walk again.
4. Not every film-actor is a star.
5. Some of the delegates failed to appear.
6. They did not tell me I could do that.

Answers to exercises on part VI

1. $\sim$ I see why the ratepayers of this Borough should finance the Council's inefficiency.
2. $\sim\left\{\begin{array}{l}\text{Some}\\ \text{Any}\end{array}\right\}$ politicians are happy.
3. $\sim$ He will (ever) walk again.
4. $\sim$ Every film-actor is a star.
5. $\sim$ All the delegates appeared.
6. $\sim$ They told me I could do that.

Part VII

VII Translating & and V

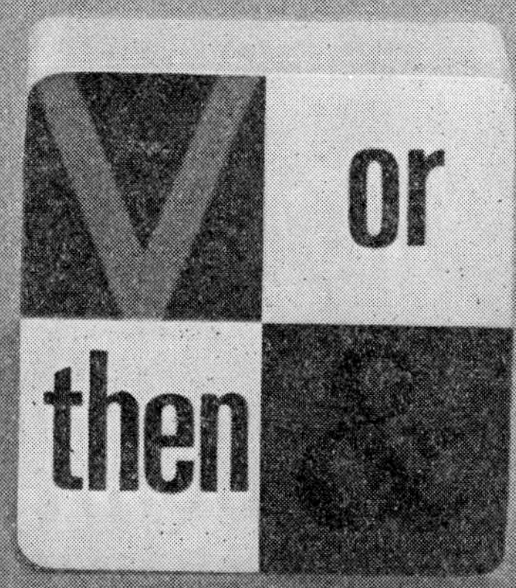

VII Translating & and V

1 Just as ~ is not just a substitute for the word "not", so & is not just a substitute for the word "and".

As in the case of ~, there are all sorts of ways of expressing the operator & in English. The best way of recognizing them is to remember that & is a *truth-functional operator*, producing a compound sentence which is true if, and only if, both the sentences joined by & are true: otherwise the compound sentence is false. *Any* expression which joins two sentences in this way will be amenable to some translation using &.

Of course, the word "and" does sometimes function as a truth-functional operator in English. Consider the sentence

John has accepted the invitation and Mary has refused.

If the two statements,

John has accepted the invitation.
Mary has refused

were both true, would

John has accepted the invitation and Mary has refused

be true?

---

2 If one or both of — Yes

John has accepted the invitation
Mary has refused

were false, would
John has accepted the invitation and Mary has refused

be true?

---

3 Would it be correct to translate the "and" in this sentence by &? — No

---

4 Write out the translation: — Yes

---

5 However, "and" is not the only word in English which functions like the operator &. Suppose either or both of the two sentences — John has accepted the invitation & Mary has refused.

John has accepted the invitation
Mary has refused

were false. Would the following sentences be true or false? (Answer "true" or "false" to each one.)

John has accepted the invitation but Mary has refused.

---

6 *John has accepted the invitation although Mary has refused.* **False**

---

7 So, just as **False**

John has accepted the invitation & Mary has refused

is false, if either or both of

John has accepted the invitation
Mary has refused

are false, so the two sentences

John has accepted the invitation but Mary has refused.
John has accepted the invitation although Mary has refused

are false, if either or both of

John has accepted the invitation
Mary has refused

are false. So the falsification conditions for a compound sentence formed by joining two sentences with "but" or "although", are the same as the falsification conditions for &.

But what about the *verification* conditions for "but" and "although", —the conditions under which sentences formed using them, are true? Are they the same as the verification conditions for &?

Suppose both of the two sentences

John has accepted the invitation
Mary has refused

are true. Would you feel this was sufficient reason for counting

John has accepted the invitation but Mary has refused
John has accepted the invitation although Mary has refused

as true?

Yes/No

If you answer "Yes" turn to frame 8a.

If you answer "No" turn to frame 8b.

8a If you answered "Yes" to the above question, then you will agree that

John has accepted the invitation & Mary has refused

is an acceptable translation of both

John has accepted the invitation but Mary has refused

and

John has accepted the invitation although Mary has refused;

and indeed this translation is regarded as acceptable by many logicians. Carry on to frame 8b below.

8b If you answered "no" to the last question, it is probably because you feel that the two sentences

John has accepted the invitation but Mary has refused
John has accepted the invitation although Mary has refused.

say rather more than just

John has accepted the invitation & Mary has refused.

In this of course you are right. But I think what we have here is another case of subtleties and nuances of meaning occurring in different expressions of ordinary language; nuances which are irrelevant to their role as truth-functional operators. The difficulties in the way of translating "but" and "although" by & are exactly analogous to the difficulties of translating

He failed to show up yesterday

as

$\sim$ *He showed up yesterday.*

If what we want from a translation is an exact rendering of every shade of meaning in the expression you are translating, the two "translations" containing $\sim$ and & are inadequate; but this is *not* why we make these translations. We make them to lay bare the *logic* of what we are translating; and any shades of meaning which do not affect the logic of the passage can safely be ignored in our translation.

Of course, cases can occur in which it is the *non*-truth-functional, rather than the truth-functional element in an expression, which plays the leading role in an argument. When this happens it will probably be pointless to translate it with a truth-functional operator. For example, the sentence

John accepted the invitation even though Mary refused

carries the suggestion that John knew about Mary's refusal of the invitation, and might have been deterred by it from accepting, but nevertheless went ahead and accepted anyway. So it is conceivable that in the appropriate situation someone might argue as follows:

John accepted the invitation even though Mary refused

....

John doesn't give a damn what Mary does.

Clearly in this argument, the *non*-truth-functional element in "even though" is paramount: one could not draw the conclusion

John doesn't give a damn what Mary does

from the premiss

John has accepted the invitation & Mary has refused

since the last premiss, with &, carries no suggestion at all that John's acceptance of the invitation has anything to do with Mary's refusal of it. It simply states the fact of John's acceptance and Mary's refusal. So your exposition of the logic of *this* particular argument would not gain from a translation of "even though" by &.

But now consider the following example:

John has accepted the invitation even though Mary refused

....

John and Mary will not both be at the party.

Do you think one could, in the appropriate circumstances, draw the conclusion

John and Mary will not both be at the party

from the premiss

John has accepted the invitation & Mary refused? Yes.

---

9 So in this example, it is the truth-functional element in "even though" which comes to the fore, and justifies translation by &.

Yes, of course one could: the appropriate circumstances being that John and Mary do what they say they'll do in answers to invitations.

There are many expressions in English which have a very important non-truth-functional element in their meaning, even if the truth-functional element in it can be represented by one or other of the operators of the sentential calculus. Consider the following sentence:

John has accepted the invitation because Mary refused.

Suppose either or both of the two sentences

John accepted the invitation
Mary refused

are false. Then would

John accepted the invitation because Mary refused False

be true or false?

---

10 So we know that if

False

John accepted the invitation because Mary refused,

is *true*, then at the very least, both

John accepted the invitation

and

Mary refused

must be true. But clearly, this alone is not sufficient to guarantee the truth of

John accepted the invitation because Mary refused,

since it still allows for the possibility that John accepted the invitation for some reason quite other than Mary's refusal—and if this were the case, then

John accepted the invitation because Mary refused

would be false. So on the whole, it is unlikely that "because" will occur in arguments in such a way that it merits translation by &—even though & correctly represents what truth-functional element "because" has in its meaning. Logical translation, like other kinds of translation, requires judgement: you cannot achieve good results just by blind application of a rigid set of rules. You must judge when to translate using sentential operators and when to leave well alone, according to the shape of the particular argument you are concerned with. In the case of & remember that *all* that "p & q" does, is state the truth of both p and q; if you are considering a premiss for translation using &, and the expression you want to translate by & carries some shade of meaning over and above its truth-functional meaning, ask yourself: Is it the truth-functional or the non-truth-functional meaning, that is important in the argument? Will the conclusion still follow from a truth-functional translation of that premiss? If not, then truth-functional translation and analysis will probably not be appropriate. If you are translating an isolated sentence out of context (doing a translation exercise, in fact!) so that you cannot judge from the context what is appropriate, ask yourself: Is it absolutely clear that the truth-functional translation of this sentence could be true, and yet the original could be false? If so, then a truth-functional translation will be inappropriate.

Which of the following sentences can be translated using &? Write out the version with & where appropriate; otherwise write "inappropriate".

I enjoyed the crossing, but my wife was sea-sick.

11 *John left for America when Mary got back from France.*

I enjoyed the crossing & my wife was sea-sick

12 *Though he is over 60, he does not have a single grey hair.*

Inappropriate: the truth-functional version would still be true if John left before Mary got back.

13 *I told him I had lost it, but he refused to believe me.*

He is over 60 & he does not have a single grey hair

14 *I made it with margarine because there is no butter left.*

I told him I had lost it & he refused to believe me

15 In which of the following arguments would a truth-functional analysis be appropriate?

Inappropriate: I might have made it with margarine because I liked it, in which case "I made it with

Ex. 42. *John flew to America yesterday because he knew Mary was coming back from France today.*

....

John is avoiding Mary.

Ex. 43. *John flew to America yesterday because he knew Mary was coming back from France today.*

....

John will have got to America before Mary finds out.

margarine because there was no butter left" would be false, though "I made it with margarine & there was no butter left" would still be true.

---

16 In Ex. 43 the causal aspect of "because" does not figure in the argument at all; the conclusion still follows if you translate "because" by &.

The particular difficulty that we have been discussing of extra dimensions of meaning in ordinary language which do not carry over to our operators, actually arises in the case of the word "and" itself. "And" in English is often used to mean "and *then*"—to indicate temporal order. A sentence such as

She opened the door and the light went out

is often, especially in narrative, used to mean

First she opened the door and then the light went out.

But there is no suggestion of temporal order in

She opened the door & the light went out.

It means exactly the same as

The light went out & she opened the door.

If we want to indicate temporal order in our translation with &, we would have to add it in specifically, e.g.

She opened the door at time t_1 & the light went out at time t_2 & time t_2 is later than time t_1.

This brings us to the other major class of translation difficulties—those arising from the fact that "and" in ordinary English has other uses than as a sentential operator. "And" unlike &, is used to join nouns, verbs and adjectives as well as sentences, e.g.

George and Mabel are going to America.

In this sentence, "and" is *not* functioning as a sentential operator So would it be correct to translate it with &, as follows:

George & Mabel are going to America.

Ex. 43.

---

17 However, this sentence can be rewritten in such a way as to produce a sentence in which "and" does occur as a sentential operator, and which means essentially the same as

George and Mabel are going to America.

Can you see what this re-written sentence would be?

No: & joins only *sentences*

---

18 So how could you translate

George and Mabel are going to America

using & ?

George is going to America and Mabel is going to America

---

19 We find "and" used to join adjectives and verbs in a similar way; e.g.:

He is rich and famous.

How would you translate this using & ?

George is going to America & Mabel is going to America.

---

20 How would you translate the following sentence, using & ?

Next week they are painting and papering the hall.

He is rich & he is famous

---

21 Sometimes the sentence may have to be rewritten in a fairly drastic and less obvious way.

Consider the following sentence:

George and Mabel are just good friends.

Would it be correct to translate it as

George & Mabel are just good friends?

Next week they are painting the hall & next week they are papering the hall.

---

22 Would it be correct to translate it as

George is just a good friend & Mabel is just a good friend?

No: & joins only *sentences*

---

23 Can you find a way of re-writing: "George and Mabel are just good friends" using & correctly?

No: because this leaves out an essential part of the meaning of the original sentence, namely that George and Mabel are good friends *of each other.*

---

24 Another example of an expression needing drastic re-writing is the expression "Neither . . . nor . . ."

Consider the sentence

Neither John nor Mary is going to the party.

This can be rewritten as a conjunction of two negations. Can you see what the two negations would be? (Write them out in words.)

George is just a good friend of Mabel & Mabel is just a good friend of George.

---

25 Now join them together with & to form the conjunction:

John is not going to the party.
Mary is not going to the party

---

26 So we translate "Neither p nor q" as "Not-p & not-q" (where p and q are sentences).

Sometimes however the "and" of ordinary English joins nouns, adjectives or adverbs in such a way that the sentence *cannot* be re-written as two sentences joined together by &. Consider the sentence

My uncle was in the Black and Tans.

Does this mean the same as

My uncle was in the Blacks and my uncle was in the Tans?

John is not going to the party & Mary is not going to the party

---

27 Would it be correct to translate it as

My uncle was in the Blacks & my uncle was in the Tans?

No

---

28 There is in fact no way of re-writing this sentence so that you can use &. The "and" occurs as part of a proper name, which cannot be broken up.

No

29 The first thing to remember about translating with v, is that v stands for the inclusive, not the exclusive "or". "p or q" means "p or q or both"; it does *not* mean "p or q but not both". v is thus not appropriate for translating uses of "or" which are clearly intended to exclude the possibility of both disjuncts being true.

Here are the two examples we considered when I was dealing with this topic in part IV. Can you remember, *without looking back to part* IV which of these two examples could be correctly translated using v?

Ex. 23a. *Either John's not as bright as we thought, or he hasn't been working.*

Ex. 23b. *The winner will get £1000 in cash or a holiday for two in Bermuda.*

If you think Ex. 23a can be translated using v: go to frame 31 on page 97.

If you think Ex. 23b can be translated using v: go to frame 30 on page 97.

30 You are wrong, I'm afraid—it is Ex. 23a which can be translated using v. "p v q" counts true if *both* p *and* q turn out to be true. Don't you agree that we would still count.

Ex. 23a. *Either John's not as bright as we thought or he hasn't been working*

as true, if we discovered that John was not bright after all, and hadn't been working either? Suppose you are one of John's teachers, and someone makes this remark (Ex. 23a) to you as he marks John's exam paper. Then you make these sad discoveries about John: he's as thick as a post and lazy with it. Would you feel justified in saying to the person who made the remark, Ex. 23a, to you, "You were wrong about John"? Wouldn't it be more appropriate, in the circumstances, to say "You were right twice over about John—he isn't bright, *and* he hasn't been working!" In other words, I claim that if both disjuncts of Ex. 23a are true, you would still count Ex. 23a as true. In the other example, however,

Ex. 23b. *The winner will get £1000 in cash or a holiday for two in Bermuda*

it is surely clear that the winner will not be allowed to claim *both* prizes. So Ex. 23a, but *not* Ex. 23b, can be translated using v, thus:

John's not as bright as we thought v *John hasn't been working.*

Now go on to frame 32 on page 98.

31 Well done: you have remembered that v stands for the *inclusive* "or". Ex. 23a can be translated using v because it allows for the possibility that John is neither bright nor working. The "or" in Ex. 23b, on the other hand, is obviously *exclusive*, since the winner will surely not get both the holiday and the cash. So it cannot be translated by v.

Now go on to frame 32 on page 98.

32 Here are two more examples:

Ex. 44. *Either he's still in prison or someone has put up bail for him.*

Ex. 45. *In his spare time he enjoys gardening or watching football on T.V.*

Which of Exs. 44 and 45 could be translated using v?

If you think the answer is Ex. 44: go to frame 33 on page 99.

If you think the answer is Ex. 45: go to frame 34 on page 99.

33 Sorry, you have got it wrong—it is Ex. 45 which can be translated by v. Here are the two examples again:

Ex. 44. *Either he's still in prison or someone has put up bail for him.*
Ex. 45. *In his spare time he enjoys gardening or watching football on T.V.*

The point of bail is to let you out of prison: so the "or" in Ex. 44 is clearly exclusive—the truth of one disjunct would automatically exclude the truth of the other. When this is so you cannot translate "or" by v. But the person referred to in Ex. 45 clearly enjoys both gardening and watching football in his spare time. So the "or" in Ex. 45 is inclusive, and can be translated by v. Perhaps you should look back at my previous explanations of this point. They are in IV 15–23, VII 29–31. When you feel confident that you have understood your mistakes so far on this point, go on to frame 35 on page 100.

34 Correct—well done, you are getting the idea. Go on to frame 35 on page 100.

From frames 33 and 34

35 Apart from this special difficulty the problems of translating with v are similar to the problems of translating with &. Once more we have the difficulty that "or" in English carries shades of meaning not present in the truth-functional meaning of v.

Joining two statements by "or" often carries the suggestion that they are connected in some way; for example, the statement

We shall operate or he will die

carries the suggestion that our operating on him may actually *prevent* him from dying. (Another way of saying this would be "He will die unless we operate".) But there is no such suggestion in

We shall operate v *he will die.*

According to the truth-table for v, this last statement would be true if at least one of its disjuncts were true, whether our operating on him could have any effect on his dying or not.

If, for example,

We shall operate

is true, then *any* disjunction of which it is a disjunct will be true regardless of whether the sentence joined to it by v—the other disjunct—has anything to do with operating or not. Thus, if

We shall operate

is true, this *in itself* is sufficient to guarantee the truth not only of

We shall operate v *he will die*

but also of

We shall operate v *he will live,*

or indeed of

We shall operate v *the duck-billed platypus is a mammal.*

For "p v q" counts as true provided that at least one of "p" and "q" are true; "p" and "q" need not have any connection with each other at all. We can say that "p v q" translates "p or q" or "p unless q" provided we remember that it is only the truth-functional aspects of "or" and "unless" that are translated by v.

Thus we can see that translating "or" by v is open to the same sorts of reservations as translating "but" and "although" by &; and it is justified in much the same way. Though "or" has additional overtones of meaning in ordinary English, as well as its truth-functional meaning, the truth-functional element is usually a sufficiently substantial part of its meaning to warrant translation by v.

Is the following sentence true or false?

2 + 2 = 4 v *4 is an odd number.*

---

36 Is the following sentence true or false?

2 + 2 = 5 v *4 is an odd number.*

True: 2 + 2 = 4 is true

---

37 Is the following sentence true or false?

There are more rats in Baltimore v *steel is a metal.*

False: both disjuncts are false.

---

38 Is the following sentence true or false?

Cats are animals v *pigeons are birds.*

True: "steel is a metal" is true

---

39 Other translation difficulties with v arise from the fact that "or", like "and", besides not being purely truth-functional, is also not solely a sentential operator: it joins single words and phrases as well as complete sentences. Again like "and", in some cases the sentence can be re-written as two sentences joined by "or" without loss or change of meaning, e.g.:

True: both disjuncts are true.

Either the valve or the transformer has gone

means the same as

Either the valve has gone or the transformer has gone

and can be translated as

The valve has gone v *the transformer has gone.*

How would you translate the following sentences, using v?

We shall visit Mexico or Peru.

---

40 *Either the road or the tyres are terribly bad.*

We shall visit Mexico v we shall visit Peru

---

41 However, it is not always possible to re-write sentences in this way.

The road is terribly bad v the tyres are terribly bad

Take for example

Ex. 46. *Jones intends to reach the summit or die in the attempt.*

Does this mean the same as the following sentence:

Ex. 47. *Jones intends to reach the summit* v *Jones intends to die in the attempt on the summit.*

If you think the two sentences *do* mean the same: go to frame 43 on page 102.

If you think the two sentences *do not* mean the same: go to frame 42 on page 102.

From frame 41

42 Correct; well done. Can you explain why not, by suggesting in the space below a situation in which one of Ex. 46 and Ex. 47 would be true and the other false?

For my suggestion, see frame 44 on page 103. Then go on to frame 45 on page 103.

From frame 41

43 Wrong; Ex. 46 and Ex. 47 do not mean the same. But don't be discouraged: this is quite a subtle point. Let me try to explain it.

Imagine that Jones is a member of an expedition which is about to make an attempt on Everest. Do the following three statements all agree over what Jones intends to do?

Ex. 48. *Jones intends to reach the summit.*
Ex. 49. *Jones intends to die in an attempt on the summit.*
Ex. 46. *Jones intends to reach the summit or die in the attempt.*

Go to frame 44 on page 103.

From frame 42

44 One can surely distinguish between these three quite different intentions: the intention to reach the summit, the intention to die while taking part in an attempt on the summit, and the intention to reach the summit or die in the attempt—i.e. to die rather than abandon the attempt on the summit.

Now look at the proposed translation again:

Ex. 46. *Jones intends to reach the summit or die in the attempt.*
Ex. 47. *Jones intends to reach the summit* v *Jones intends to die in the attempt on the summit.*

Ex. 47 attributes either of the first two of the three intentions (listed in frame 43) to Jones: it states that either Ex. 48 or Ex. 49 or both are true. Ex. 46 attributes the third of the three intentions to him—and we have agreed that this third intention is quite different from the other two. Ex. 47 would be true if Jones was bent on suicide and intended to die during an attempt on the summit, even if he himself has no firm intention of actually reaching the summit. But if *that* were the case—if Jones has no serious intention of going for the summit—then "Jones intends to reach the summit or die in the attempt", Ex. 46, would surely count as false. Here we have a situation where Ex. 47 counts as true, and Ex. 46 counts as false; so clearly the two examples cannot mean the same.

Now go on to frame 45 below.

45 Sometimes it may be quite difficult to tell if v is the appropriate translation for "or". Consider now the sentence

Ex. 50. *Jones will reach the summit or die in the attempt.*

We can read this sentence in two ways: first, as a way of telling us about the degree of Jones's determination to reach the summit; and the second, as a straightforward prediction of the two things that are likely to happen to Jones. If we read it as being about Jones's determination to reach the summit, do you think it would be right to translate it as

Jones will reach the summit v *Jones will die in the attempt?*

If you think the translation *would* be correct: go to frame 46 on page 104.

If you think the translation would *not* be correct: go to frame 47 on page 104.

From frame 45

46 Wrong; but don't be down-hearted—this really is quite a difficult philosophical point.

If Ex. 50 is about Jones's determination to reach the summit, the "or" must be functioning in the same way as the "or" in "Jones intends to reach the summit or die in the attempt" (Ex. 46); in fact, I think the two sentences come to much the same thing. So if we read Ex. 50 as being about Jones's determination to reach the summit, we should not translate the "or" by v for the same reasons as applied to Ex. 46. For these, go back to frame 43 on page 102.

When you think you have got this point, go on to frame 48 on page 102.

From frame 45

47 Very good; you are right. Ex. 50 really comes to much the same thing as Ex. 46, and cannot be translated by v for the same reasons. Go on to frame 48.

From frames 46 and 47

48 Suppose now we read

Ex. 50. *Jones will reach the summit or die in the attempt.*

as a straightforward factual prediction of the two things that are likely to happen to Jones. In this case, would be Ex. 50 be translated by

Jones will reach the summit v *Jones will die in the attempt?*

If you think it *would* be so translatable go to frame 50 on page 106.

If you think it would *not* be so translatable go to frame 49 on page 106.

From frame 49

49 Wrong, I'm afraid—this is one of the cases where the issue is *not* confused by a tacit reference to Jones's intention. A prediction that one of two things will happen will clearly be satisfied by one or other of them in fact happening. So if we read Ex. 50 as the prediction that either Jones will reach the summit or Jones will die in the attempt, this prediction will be a true prediction if Jones reaches the summit, and it will be a true prediction if Jones dies in the attempt. Indeed we would probably regard it as a true prediction if *both* things happened—if Jones expired at the moment of reaching the summit. These are exactly the truth-conditions for v.

Now go on to frame 51 on page 107.

From frame 49

50 Correct. Move on to frame 51 on page 107.

51 Are the following sentences

(a) translatable using v;

(b) not translatable using v;

(c) translatable using v, under one interpretation, but not translatable using v, under another interpretation? Supply the translation where possible.

Ex. 51. *She wants to go to Greece or Yugoslavia.*

---

52 Ex. 52. *I saw him on Tuesday or Wednesday.*

(b) This sentence is like "Jones intends to reach the summit or die in the attempt".

---

53 Ex. 53. *We will go to San Francisco or bust.*

(a) I saw him on Tuesday v I saw him on Wednesday

---

54 Ex. 54. *Theirs not to reason why*
Theirs but to do or die.

(b) I personally can't regard "we will bust" as a serious prediction. If you can, then "We will go to San Francisco v we will bust" is all right, and the answer would be (c).

55

(b) They have a complex duty to "do or die" which can't be split up—see Ex. 46 and Ex. 51.

Exercises on &

Re-write the following sentences, where possible, using &. Write "impossible" where appropriate. Restrict yourself to one operator per sentence.

1. He has published three novels and a collection of poems.
2. John, but not Mary, has accepted the invitation.
3. I told him to go and jump in the lake.
4. He does neither the one thing nor the other.
5. He did not remember to call, although I reminded him.
6. I want a black and white cat.
7. I believe neither the defence nor the prosecution.
8. I did it because I was afraid.
9. We have written all the envelopes, but we haven't filled them.
10. He can sing and play the accordion.

1. He has published three novels & he has published a collection of poems.
2. John has accepted the invitation & Mary has not accepted the invitation.
3. Impossible: I would count "go and jump in the lake" as a single idiom which cannot sensibly be broken up, i.e. I don't think 3. does mean the same as "I told him to go & I told him to jump in the lake".
4. He does not do the one thing & he does not do the other (thing).
5. He did not remember to call & I reminded him to call.
6. Impossible. 6. clearly does not mean the same as "I want a black cat & I want a white cat", which implies I want *two* cats.
7. I do not believe the defence & I do not believe the prosecution.
8. Impossible. 8. could be false when "I did it & I was afraid" was true.
9. We have written all the envelopes & { We haven't filled all the envelopes / We have filled none of the envelopes. }

   Which of the two alternatives you choose for the second conjunction depends on how you interpret "we haven't filled them".
10. He can sing & he can play the accordion.

Part VIII

VIII Translating →

Part VIII

VIII Translating $\rightarrow$

1 We have already (in part V) dealt with one of the major difficulties with translating $\rightarrow$; the difficulty that "if . . . then . . .", like "or", usually joins sentences which are connected in some way, while $\rightarrow$ and v, being purely truth-functional, can join sentences which are totally unconnected and still produce a true statement. Thus, you will remember, all the following statements count as true:

France is in America $\rightarrow$ *cats are animals*
Sweden is in America $\rightarrow$ *pigs can fly*
France is in Europe $\rightarrow$ *water is wet.*

Although it is in a way misleading to translate the above sentences as, respectively,

If France is in America then cats are animals
If Sweden is in America then pigs can fly
If France is in Europe then water is wet

because of the causal implications which usually attach to "if . . . then . . .", nevertheless this still seems to be the best and simplest available way of translating them, because of the affinities that do exist between $\rightarrow$ and "if . . . then . . ." (see part V). The trouble is that, as with the other operators, there is no exact idiomatic English equivalent of $\rightarrow$. The nearest English equivalents still say or imply more than is contained in $\rightarrow$. But as long as we remain aware of this, translating $\rightarrow$ by "if . . . then . . ." need not lead us into error.

There are however ample other opportunities for error in translating $\rightarrow$, some major, some minor. Let us clear up the minor ones first before tackling the major problems.

The minor difficulties with translating $\rightarrow$, are connected with verbs in "if . . . then . . ." statements. English sometimes alters the future to the present tense after "if": we might say

Ex. 55. *If she's cooking, I shall stay*

when what we mean is

Ex. 56. *If she is going to cook, I shall stay.*

But sometimes we may want to distinguish the conditional containing the present tense from the conditional containing the future; i.e. between Ex. 55 meaning the same as Ex. 56, and between

Ex. 57. *If she is (now in the act of) cooking, I shall stay.*

When translating with $\rightarrow$, we should change a present tense in the antecedent to the future in those cases where a future action or event is clearly meant, for we might not otherwise be able to distinguish our translation from a translation of a conditional like Ex. 55. So we should translate Ex. 56 like this:

She is going to cook → I shall stay.

And we should translate Ex. 57 like this:

She is cooking → I shall stay.

If we translate Ex. 55 like this:

She's cooking → I shall stay

there could be some doubt as to whether Ex. 56 or Ex. 57 was intended.

Another thing to watch for, is that "if . . . then . . ." statements containing subjunctive verbs cannot be translated by → at all. Consider the sentence

If he were to come, I should go.

This cannot be translated by

He were to come → I should go

because "he were to come" is not a complete sentence; and there is no way of altering the verb to make it a complete sentence, which does not also change its meaning. For

If he were to come, I should go

clearly does not mean the same as

If he comes, I shall go.

Translate the following sentences using → where possible. If the sentence cannot be so translated, write "impossible":

If you go to Harvard next year you will meet my cousin.

---

2 *If I had known your cousin was going to be in Harvard, I would never have gone there.*

You go to Harvard next year → you will meet my cousin. (It is not necessary to change the tense here since the inclusion of the date, "next year", makes it obvious that a future tense is intended).

---

3 *If he digs up that rose I shall never forgive him.*

Impossible: "I had known your cousin was going to be in Harvard" does not make sense on its own.

---

4 The major difficulty with translating → is the variety of confusing ways in which English uses "if". There are five main cases to distinguish:

If p, then q
p if q.

He will dig up that rose → I shall never forgive him.

Only if p, (then) q
p only if q
p if and only if q.

All of these uses of "if" can be translated by →: but they are not all translated in the same way. The correct translation for all of them is is *not* p → q.

Consider first "if p then q" and "p if q". We have already mentioned this point—that English commonly reverses the order in which antecedent and consequent of a conditional occur in a sentence: we may say either

Ex. 58. *If John has told the police, then Mary is in danger*

or

Ex. 59. *Mary is in danger if John has told the police.*

This possibility disguises the fact that the two versions mean exactly the same thing truth-functionally, and should both be translated by

Ex. 60. *John has told the police → Mary is in danger.*

Now put "p" for "John has told the police", and "q" for "Mary is in danger" in Ex. 58, Ex. 59 and Ex. 60 above. What do you get for Ex. 58?

If p then q

5 What do you get for Ex. 59?

---

q if p

6 What do you get for Ex. 60?

---

p → q

7 So we see that both the sentences

If p then q
q if p

are translated by

p → q.

Now, if the sentence

q if p

is translated by

p → q

how would you translate the sentence

p if q?

---

q → p

8 How would you translate the sentence

If the gas-ring lights automatically, then the pilot light is on?

---

9 How would you translate the sentence

The gas-ring lights automatically if the pilot light is on?

The gas-ring lights automatically → the pilot light is on.

---

10 So this is the first trap to beware of when translating sentences containing "if": a sentence of the form

If p then q

is translated

$p \rightarrow q$

but a sentence of the form

p if q

is translated

$q \rightarrow p$

What is the antecedent of the conditional

$q \rightarrow p$?

The pilot light is on → the gas-ring lights automatically.

---

11 So what is the antecedent of the conditional

p if q?

q

---

12 What is the antecedent of the conditional

$p \rightarrow q$?

q

---

13 So what is the antecedent of the conditional

If p then q?

p

---

14 What is the consequent of the conditional

$q \rightarrow p$?

p

---

15 So what is the consequent of the conditional

p if q?

p

---

16 What is the consequent of the conditional

$p \rightarrow q$?

p

---

17 So what is the consequent of the conditional

if p then q?

---

18 So you can see that the difference between the two sentences

q

if p then q
p if q

is that, though both are translatable using $\rightarrow$, the two sentences each represent a different conditional; for the antecedent of the one is the consequent of the other, and the consequent of one is the antecedent of the other. Sorting out the differences between "if p then q", "p if q", "p only if q" "p if and only if q" means sorting out which of "p" and "q" is the antecedent and which the consequent in each case.

Fortunately there is a fairly quick and simple way of doing this. Look at the truth-table for $\rightarrow$ again:

$T \rightarrow T = T$
$T \rightarrow F = F$
$F \rightarrow T = T$
$F \rightarrow F = T$

You can see from this truth-table that there is only one combination of truth-values for antecedent and consequent that falsifies a conditional. Which is it?

True antecedent, true consequent;
True antecedent, false consequent;
False antecedent, true consequent;
False antecedent, false consequent.

---

19 This gives us a way of determining the antecedent and consequent of any conditional, no matter how confusingly it is expressed in English. If we can decide for any conditional what combination of truth-values for its constituent sentences would falsify it, we will know that the *true* sentence of that falsifying combination is the antecedent and the *false* sentence is the consequent of the conditional. So we will know that the sentence can be translated using $\rightarrow$, by writing the *true* sentence of the falsifying combination to the left of the $\rightarrow$, and the *false* sentence of the falsifying combination to the right of the $\rightarrow$. (If the falsifying combination does *not* consist of one true and one false sentence, we shall know that the apparent conditional should not be translated by $\rightarrow$ at all.)

True antecedent, false consequent.

Let us see how this works with the case we have already considered: p if q. Consider the conditional

The gas-ring lights automatically if the pilot light is on

Which of the following situations would make this conditional false?

The gas-ring lighting automatically with the pilot light on

The gas-ring not lighting automatically with the pilot light on

The gas-ring lighting automatically with the pilot light off

The gas-ring not lighting automatically with the pilot light off.

---

20 So our conditional, "The gas-ring lights automatically if the pilot light is on", will be *false* if the gas-ring doesn't light automatically when the pilot light is on.

Now, the constituent sentences of our conditional are:

The gas-ring lights automatically
The pilot light is on.

Which of these two sentences will be *true*, in the situation which makes our conditional *false*?

The gas-ring not lighting automatically with the pilot light on

---

21 Which of the two constituent sentences would be *false*, in the situation which makes our conditional *false*?

The pilot light is on

---

22 The combination of the *true* sentence, "The pilot light is on", with the *false* sentence "The gas-ring lights automatically" is what I call the *falsifying combination* for the conditional, "The gas-ring lights automatically if the pilot light is on": it is the combination of the two sentences, one true and one false, which describe the situation which falsifies the conditional.

We know from the truth-table for $\rightarrow$ that a conditional is false only if its antecedent is true and its consequent false. So the *true* sentence of the falsifying combination for "The gas-ring lights automatically if the pilot light is on", must be the antecedent of that conditional; and the *false* sentence of the falsifying combination must be its consequent. So what is the antecedent of the conditional

The gas-ring lights automatically if the pilot light is on?

The gas-ring lights automatically

---

23 What is the consequent of the same conditional?

The pilot light is on

---

24 So how would we write

The gas-ring lights automatically if the pilot light is on

using $\rightarrow$?

The gas-ring lights automatically

---

25 Now let us take a new sentence-form:

p only if q

and a new example. Consider the sentence

The Royal standard flies only if the Queen is in residence

What this sentence states is that the *only* occasion on which the Royal standard flies, is when the Queen is in residence. Clearly, it will be falsified if the Royal standard flies on any other occasion. So which of the following situations would falsify it?

The Royal standard flying with the Queen in residence

The Royal standard not flying with the Queen in residence

The Royal standard flying with the Queen not in residence

The Royal standard not flying with the Queen not in residence.

The pilot light is on → the gas-ring lights automatically

---

26 What are the two constituent sentences of "The Royal standard flies only if the Queen is in residence"?

The Royal standard flying with the Queen not in residence

---

27 So what is the falsifying combination for "The Royal standard flies only if the Queen is in residence"? (State which is the true sentence of the falsifying combination, and which the false).

"The Royal standard flies (or is flying)" and "The Queen is in residence."

---

28 So which is the antecedent of the conditional "The Royal standard flies only if the Queen is in residence"?

The Royal standard is flying—true
The Queen is in residence—false

---

29 Which is the consequent of the same conditional?

The Royal standard flies (is flying)

---

30 So how would you write

The Royal standard flies only if the Queen is in residence

using →?

The Queen is in residence

---

31 So the sentence-form

p only if q

is translated

The Royal standard flies (is flying) → the Queen is in residence

$p \to q$.

Now let us take the conditional:

Only if p, (then) q.

Consider the sentence

Only if there are candidates from all the parties are we voting.

What are the two constituent sentences of this conditional?

---

32 What is the falsifying combination for this conditional? (State which is the true sentence of the falsifying combination and which the false).

There are candidates from all the parties
We are voting

---

33 So what is the antecedent of the conditional "Only if there are candidates from all the parties are we voting"?

We are voting—true
There are candidates from all the parties—false

---

34 What is the consequent of the same conditional?

We are voting

---

35 So how would you write

Only if there are candidates from all the parties are we voting

using $\to$?

There are candidates from all the parties

---

36 So the sentence form "Only if p, (then) q" is translated

$q \to p$

Let us summarize our results so far:

If p then q	$= p \to q$
p if q	$= q \to p$
p only if q	$= p \to q$
Only if p, q	$= q \to p$

Thus we see that the four English expressions we have considered so far divide into two pairs which are truth-functionally equivalent in meaning—they have the same translation using $\to$.

Which is the English expression equivalent to

If p then q

We are voting $\to$ there are candidates from all the parties

---

37 Which is the English expression equivalent to

p if q?

p only if q

---

38 So we can summarize our results as follows:

Only if p, q

if p then q $=$ p $\rightarrow$ q $=$ p only if q
p if q $=$ q $\rightarrow$ p $=$ only if p, q.

One further word of warning about "only if". English often separates the "only" and the "if":

Ex. 61. *The gas-ring only lights automatically if the pilot light is on.*

Which of the following sentences is Ex. 61 above equivalent to?

Ex. 62. *Only if the gas-ring lights automatically is the pilot light on.*

Ex. 63. *The gas-ring lights automatically only if the pilot light is on.*

---

39 So how would you write

Ex. 63: The gas-ring lights automatically only if the pilot light is on

The gas-ring only lights automatically if the pilot light is on

using $\rightarrow$?

---

40 Another warning: "only if" must not be confused with "if only". "Only if" is a logical operator whose workings we have just been considering. "If only" is usually a rhetorical flourish which adds extra expressive emphasis to a sentence. Compare the two sentences:

The gas-ring lights automatically $\rightarrow$ the pilot light is on

Ex. 64. *Things will right themselves only if he comes back.*
Ex. 65. *Things would right themselves if only he came back.*

The antecedent of Ex. 64 is

Things will right themselves.

The antecedent of Ex. 65 is

he came back.

In fact, "if only" usually occurs in sentences such as Ex. 65, with subjunctive verbs, which are not in any case translatable by $\rightarrow$. So you do not need to worry too much about the antecedents and consequents of sentences containing "if only", provided that you don't confuse it with "only if".

Now let us consider the expression

p if and only if q.

(Logicians often abbreviate the awkward phrase "if and only if" to "if" spelt with two f's: "iff", and write, instead of "p if and only if q", p iff q.)

Clearly this consists of *two* conditionals:

p if q
p only if q.

How do we write

p if q

using $\rightarrow$?

$q \rightarrow p$

41 How do we write

p only if q

using $\rightarrow$?

$p \rightarrow q$

42 So

p iff q

consists of *both* of the two conditionals

$p \rightarrow q$
$q \rightarrow p$.

In the first of these two conditionals, the arrow points from the p to the q; in the second, from the q to the p. We can utilize this convenient symmetry by inventing a new symbol for "iff", a double-headed arrow, thus:

$p \leftrightarrow q$.

This means "p if and only if q", or "if p then q, and if q then p".

Now let us consider the expression

If and only if p, q.

Which two conditionals does this consist of?

If p, then q
Only if p, q

43 How are these conditionals translated using $\rightarrow$?

$p \rightarrow q$
$q \rightarrow p$

44 How were the two conditionals in

p iff q

translated, using $\rightarrow$?

$q \rightarrow p$
$p \rightarrow q$

45 What do you notice about the translations of

p iff q
Iff p, q

using $\rightarrow$?

They are the same

46 So *both* of the two expressions

Iff p then q
p iff q

are translated

$p \leftrightarrow q$.

Two of the following three statements are translated in the same way, using →. Which are they?

Ex. 66. *If Michael mows the lawn, then Wilfred weeds the flowerbeds.*
Ex. 67. *If Wilfred weeds the flowerbeds, then Michael mows the lawn.*
Ex. 68. *Wilfred weeds the flowerbeds if Michael mows the lawn.*

---

47 How would you translate Ex. 66 and Ex. 68 using →?

Ex. 66 and Ex. 68. If you got anything else, re-read VIII frames 4–18

---

48 Two of the following three statements mean the same truth-functionally. Which are they?

Ex. 69. *Wilfred weeds the flowerbeds if Michael mows the lawn.*
Ex. 70. *Only if Wilfred weeds the flowerbeds does Michael mow the lawn.*
Ex. 71. *Wilfrid weeds the flowerbeds only if Michael mows the lawn.*

Michael mows the lawn →
Wilfred weeds the flowerbeds

---

49 How would you translate Ex. 69 and Ex. 70 using →?

Ex. 69 and Ex. 70. If you get anything else, re-read VIII frames 18–31

---

50 Which of the following three statements mean the same truth functionally?

Ex. 72. *Iff Michael mows the lawn then Wilfrid weeds the flowerbeds.*
Ex. 73. *Michael mows the lawn iff Wilfrid weeds the flowerbeds.*
Ex. 74. *Michael mows the lawn only if Wilfrid weeds the flowerbeds.*

Michael mows the lawn →
Wilfred weeds the flowerbeds

---

51 How would you translate Ex. 72 and Ex. 73?

Ex. 72 and Ex. 73. If you got anything else, re-read VIII frames 40–46

52

Michael mows the lawn ↔
Wilfred weeds the flowerbeds
OR
Michael mows the lawn →
Wilfred weeds the flowerbeds, and
Wilfred weeds the flowerbeds →
Michael mows the lawn,
OR
Wilfred weeds the flowerbeds ↔
Michael mows the lawn

Exercises on part VIII

Translate the following sentences using →, where possible. If the sentences cannot be translated using →, write "impossible".

1. If it were not so, I would have told you.
2. Savings equals investments if and only if there is no private hoarding of wealth.
3. He does it if I tell him to.
4. Only if the weather breaks will we lose this election.
5. You would receive all your former status if only you would recant.
6. They only negotiate if they think you will give in.

Answers to exercises on part VIII

1. Impossible; subjunctive. "If it were not so" is not a complete sentence.
2. Savings equals investments$\leftrightarrow$there is no private hoarding of wealth.

   or

   Savings equals investments $\rightarrow$ there is no private hoarding of wealth, and there is no private hoarding of wealth $\rightarrow$ saving equals investments.
3. I tell him to (do it) $\rightarrow$ he does it.
4. We are going to lose this election $\rightarrow$ the weather is going to break.
5. Impossible: subjunctive. "You would receive all your former status" does not make complete sense (of the required kind) on its own.
6. They negotiate $\rightarrow$ they think you will give in.

Part IX

IX Notation

Part IX

IX Notation

1 One of our main tools in the study of logic is the use of logical notation: writing down arguments in symbols instead of words, so that their logical form shows up clearly.

People are often alarmed by the introduction of symbols and technical language; you may wonder why this step is necessary. Why can we not stick to ordinary language to do our logic in? Well, we could do this; but you would probably find the logic rather harder to do. The point of using symbols is to make life easier for you, not more difficult, as some of you may fear!

Think how much more difficult arithmetic, say, would be, if you had to use words instead of symbols. If you are unconvinced, try doing this sum without writing down any figures or symbols at all:

What is the sum of: the remainder from two hundred and fourteen after the subtraction of sixty-eight; and the product of three and (multiplied by) fourteen?

---

2 Did you get it right? Whether you did or not, check my arithmetic on the sum written out in figures: **One hundred and eighty-eight**

$(214 - 68) + (3 \times 14)$.

Don't you find it considerably easier to work with figures? Of course, part of the reason for this is just habit; we aren't used to adding and subtracting and multiplying in words. But it is not *just* a matter of habit. Some symbols are definitely easier to handle than others: the Romans used an extremely cumbersome set of numerals, and it seems no accident that mathematics was *not* one of the areas in which they made much progress. And it was not until after the Arabic numerals which we now use were introduced into Europe, that European mathematics really got off the ground: though the use of the Arabic system was clearly not the sole cause of the advance—the introduction of a sign for zero was also obviously very important—it does seem to have contributed to it.

A good notation is a great aid to thought. Notice that when we represent the sum using numerals instead of words for numbers, symbols instead of verbs for the operations of adding, multiplying and subtracting, and brackets for punctuation, it is clear at a glance which operations are required, and also which should be done first. The notation actually guides you towards solving the problem. This is certainly not so with the sum written down in words: you have to read right through to the end of a very long sentence before you can be sure what you are being asked to do, let alone see what is the best way to tackle it. Logic in symbols is easier than logic in words for very similar reasons; once you have got used to this new language, you will find that you can read it as easily as words.

The sort of advantage I have just been describing results largely from the different visual impact of symbols as against words. But they have other advantages to offer as well. Words in ordinary language are notoriously ambiguous; people use the same word to mean all sorts of different things. This easily leads to confusion of thought and misunderstandings. This multiplicity of meanings arises from the fact that language is built up gradually over a period of time by the habits of language users—it grows organically, as one might say. Symbol systems, on the other hand, are artificial creations: a particular set of symbols is chosen, and their meanings are arbitrarily fixed by decree, so to speak, ruling out any possibility of ambiguity. Similarly, the precise rules for the use and combination of the symbols with each other—their grammar and syntax—are arbitrarily laid down. All this arbitrariness is in aid of clarity: the rules help to keep track of exactly what we are doing at every stage of an argument, so that if an infringement occurs, it is immediately obvious both that it is an infringement, and which rule has been infringed. In short, the use of precise rules and symbols should help you to recognize and classify offences against the particular system of logic we are studying.

At this point the question arises of whether an offence against a particular system of logic is an offence against logic. Is our system the right one—in the sense of being the one we normally operate with in ordinary language—or the only one, or the only possible one? Does it have anything to do with what goes on in ordinary language at all? This is an important issue of great philosophical interest which I cannot begin to do justice to here; though the question has been raised, in an oblique way, in the five preceding parts on translation. I tried to suggest there that whatever might be the exact relation of the operators to the sentential calculus to expressions of ordinary language, at the very least it seems undeniable that certain parallels do exist. What you make of these parallels is up to you: you may regard them merely as parallels of limited interest between a natural, complex system (natural language and natural inference) and an artificially constructed, simple one (a particularly formal system of logic). Or you may go the whole hog in the opposite direction and regard logic as the final revelation of what actually goes on under the surface of natural language. I cannot attempt to go into these burning issues within the scope of this course; I can only present you with a first glimpse of a particular system and leave you to make up your own mind about its relevance or irrelevance to anything else. (If the question keeps you awake at night, it means that you are a born philosopher!)

We have already learnt symbols for the sentential operators and have occasionally substituted letters for the sentences or parts of sentences which cannot be represented by the operators. This week we shall learn the exact rules for the use of the notation we have introduced informally.

3 Our first task is to tidy up our use of letters for the parts of sentences not represented by the operator symbols. We have been writing sentence forms such as

if p then q

or

All A are B

instead of sentences like

If Stalin was a Communist, then I'm a Dutchman

or

All swans are white.

We have been using capitals from the beginning of the alphabet (A, B, C . . .) to represent non-logical parts of arguments, when these are not complete sentences. We have been using small letters from the middle of the alphabet (p, q, r . . .) to represent complete sentences.

This difference in the letters we use corresponds to the difference between the two kinds of logical words, which I pointed out at the beginning of part IV. So we shall continue to use letters to represent parts of arguments in this way, but from now on we shall do so consciously and systematically. We shall use small letters p, q, r . . . to stand for complete sentences, and capitals A, B, C . . . to stand for terms (such as "swans" and "white"). The small letters p, q, r . . . may be used to stand for *any* complete sentence (including one that contains a sentential operator) though for obvious reasons we shall mainly be using them for sentences which contain no operator. Small letters used in this way are called **sentential variables** or **sentential letters**: "sentential" because they stand for sentences, and "variables" because the sentence they stand for may vary from argument to argument. However, we must keep the *same* sentence letter for the same sentence throughout a particular argument or context.

Sentential variables
Sentence letters

Now that we have symbols for operators and letters for sentences, you will find that in the examples whose logic we study, no words appear at all. (You can now perhaps begin to see why in the Introduction I compared logic to mathematics!) To avoid confusion, from now on when we talk about a sentence written out entirely in symbols with no words appearing in it at all, we shall refer to it as a **formula.** The plural of "formula" is *formulae,* but the anglicized version *formulas* is also used.

Formula

Using "p" for "The police inspector is baffled", "q" for "The crime was committed before midnight", "r" for "John has an alibi", "s" for "Mary is lying", translate the following argument into formulae:

(a) The police inspector is baffled.
(b) If the crime was committed before midnight, then John has an alibi.
(c) The crime was committed before midnight or Mary is lying.

(d) Mary is not lying.
(e) The crime was committed before midnight.
(f) John has an alibi.
(g) John has an alibi and the police inspector is baffled.

---

4 Well-formed formulae

Though we are now writing in symbols instead of words, the grammatical rules about the formation of sentences still apply. Consider the following formula:

p & (p stands for: Stalin was a Communist).

How would you translate it into words?

(a) p
(b) q → r
(c) q v s
(d) ∼ s
(e) q
(f) r
(g) r & p

---

5 Does

Stalin was a Communist and

make complete sense on its own?

Yes/No.

Stalin was a Communist and

---

6 Well, just as

Stalin was a Communist and

does not make complete sense on its own so

p &

does not make complete sense on its own. Just as "and" requires two sentences here to complete the sense, so the symbol & requires two variables (or formulae) to complete its sense. Corresponding to the grammatical rules for the construction of sentences in English we have formation rules for the construction of symbols into formulae. The counterpart in symbols of a grammatically correct sentence in words is called a **well-formed formula** (or **wff** for short). A well-formed formula is one that makes complete sense on its own.

The formation rules for constructing wffs are as follows:
(i) A sentence letter on its own, such as

p

No

Well-formed formula wff

is a wff. "p" on its own represents a complete sentence such as "Stalin was a Communist" or "Mary loves Harry". As such, it counts as making complete sense on its own, and is a wff.

(ii) *Rule for* $\sim$: (a) the sign $\sim$ must always appear to the *left* of the variable or formula on which it operates; (b) since $\sim$ is a unary operator, one and only one variable formula must appear to the right of the sign $\sim$; (c) the variable or formula which appears to the right of the sign $\sim$ must be a wff.

Is

$\sim$

a wff?

Yes/No.

---

7 Is — No

$p \sim$

a wff?

Yes/No.

---

8 Is — No

$p \sim q$

a wff?

Yes/No.

---

9 Is — No

r

a wff?

Yes/No.

---

10 Is — Yes

$\sim r$

a wff?

Yes/No.

---

11 Is

$\sim pq$

a wff?

Yes/No.

Yes

---

12 (iii) *Rule for* &: (a) each conjunction must contain two and only two conjuncts, one to the left and one to the right of the sign &; (b) each conjunct must be a wff.

Is

p &

a wff?

Yes/No.

No

---

13 Is

p & q

a wff?

Yes/No.

No

---

14 Is

pq & r

a wff?

Yes/No.

Yes

---

15 Is

&

a wff?

Yes/No.

No

---

16 Is

& p &

a wff?

Yes/No.

No

---

17 Is

$\sim p$ &

a wff?

Yes/No.

No

---

18 Is

p & $\sim$

a wff?

Yes/No.

No

---

19 (iv) *Rule for* v: (a) each disjunction must contain two and only two disjuncts, one to the left and one to the right of the sign v; (b) each disjunct must be a wff.

Is

v

a wff?

Yes/No.

No

---

20 Is

p v &

a wff?

Yes/No.

No

---

21 Is

p v q

a wff?

Yes/No.

No

---

22 Is

r v p

a wff?

Yes/No.

Yes

---

23 Is

p v & *q*

a wff?

Yes/No.

Yes

---

24 Is

p v *r* v *q*

a wff?

Yes/No.

No

---

25 Is

v *p*

a wff?

Yes/No.

No

---

26 (v) *Rule for* →: (a) Each conditional must have one antecedent and one consequent; (b) the antecedent must appear to the *left* of the sign →, the consequent to the *right* of the sign →; (c) both antecedent and consequent must be wffs.

Is

→ *p*

a wff?

Yes/No.

No

---

27 Is

→

a wff?

Yes/No.

No

---

28 Is

q

a wff?

Yes/No.

No

---

29 Is

$q \rightarrow s$

a wff?

Yes/No.

Yes

---

30 Is

$\rightarrow q \rightarrow s$

a wff?

Yes/No.

Yes

---

31 Is

$p \rightarrow \rightarrow q$

a wff?

Yes/No.

No

---

32 (v) *Rule for* $\leftrightarrow$: One and only one wff must appear to the left of the sign $\leftrightarrow$, and one and only one wff must appear to the right of the sign $\leftrightarrow$.

Is

$p \leftrightarrow$

a wff?

Yes/No.

No

---

33 Is

$pq \leftrightarrow qr$

a wff?

Yes/No.

No

---

34 Is

$p \leftrightarrow q$

a wff?

Yes/No.

No

---

35 Is Yes

$q \leftrightarrow q$

a wff?

Yes/No.

---

36 Is Yes

$\& \leftrightarrow \&$

a wff?

Yes/No.

---

37 Is No

$\leftrightarrow p$

a wff?

Yes/No.

---

38 Punctuation: Brackets No

So far we have dealt mainly with sentences containing one sentential operator each, such as

If Stalin was a Communist then I'm a Dutchman

which contains the operator "if . . . then . . .", or

George is not going to fire Harry

which contains the sentential operator "not". But a sentence containing a sentential operator is itself a complete sentence, and as such can have another sentential operator applied to it: for example,

If George is not going to fire Harry, then Mary will divorce him.

This sentence contains *two* sentential operators—"not" and "if . . . then". This possibility raises problems for our symbolic notation. Suppose we start with the sentential variable "p", standing for a simple sentence—that is, one containing no sentential operator—say, "Mary is John's ex-wife". Let us put it in a box, thus:

p

You may remember from part II that the box signifies a *sentence.* I put the variable "p" into a box in order to make absolutely clear that it stands for a *complete sentence,* which can be operated on by a sentential operator—such as &. Of course, since & is a binary operator, we will need another sentential variable as well—say "q", standing for "Mary is engaged to Harry". We put "q" into a box, thus:

q

and then join the two variables together with &:

p & q (Read: p and q)

If "p" stands for "Mary is John's ex-wife" and "q" stands for "Mary is engaged to Harry", what will

p & q

stand for?

---

39 This is again a whole new sentence, which can also be put into a sentence-box, thus:

[p & q]

and have another operator applied to it—say →. Of course, since → requires two sentences to complete its sense, we shall also have to supply another sentential variable to go with it; say

r

standing for

John will be furious.

We can use this in combination with → and

[p & q]

to obtain

[p & q] → r (if p and q, then r)

This stands for a complete new sentence—a conditional. What would it be?

Mary is John's ex-wife and (Mary is) engaged to Harry.

---

40 This conditional is still grammatical—well-formed in ordinary language. And the process need not end here; this new conditional could itself go into a sentence-box, and have another operator applied to it—the tilde, say—to form yet another new sentence—a negation. Can you draw this one yourself? (Just the box the last formula arrived at and add the ~.)

If Mary is John's ex-wife and (Mary is) engaged to Harry, then John will be furious.

---

41 And what would this new formula stand for, or mean?

Ex. 75

$$\sim \boxed{\boxed{\boxed{p} \;\&\; \boxed{q}} \;\to\; \boxed{r}}$$

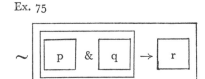

42 We could go on adding boxes and operators indefinitely: there is in principle no necessary limit to this process. But let us stop here and consider another set of boxes. We'll start this time with the variable "p" (still standing for "Mary is John's ex-wife") box it, and apply the tilde to it:

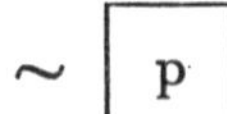

What would this mean?

It is not the case that if Mary is John's ex-wife and Mary is engaged to Harry, then John will be furious.

---

43 Now we take the variables "q" (still standing for "Mary is engaged to Harry") and "r" (still standing for "John will be furious"); each of these is a complete sentence, so each can be boxed, and the two joined together with → to form the conditional:

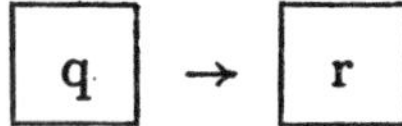

What would this mean?

Mary is not John's ex-wife.

---

44 The negation and the conditional that we have just obtained are again both complete sentences. So again each can be boxed:

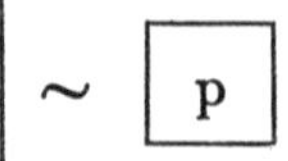

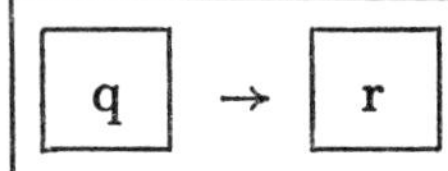

and the two can be joined together with & to form the conjunction

Ex. 76.

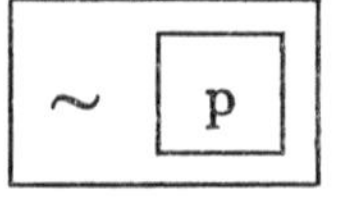

&

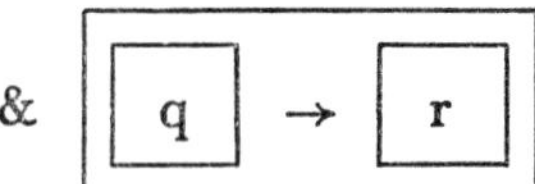

What would this mean?

If Mary is engaged to Harry, then John will be furious

---

45 Here are the two sets of boxes, side by side:

Ex. 75.

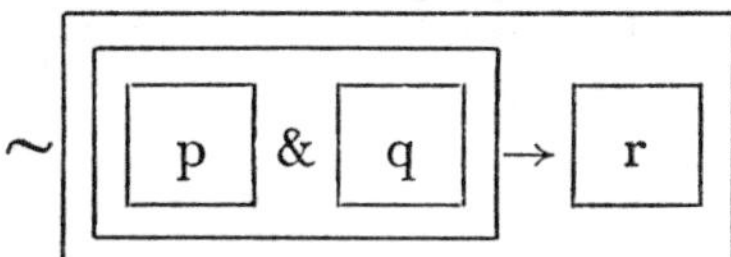

Ex. 76

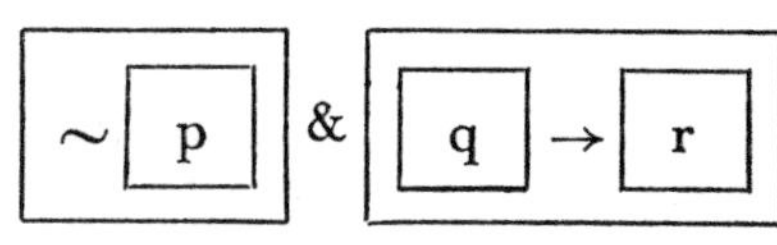

what happens if we *remove* the boxes? Write out the two strings of symbols which result:

Mary is not John's ex-wife, and if Mary is engaged to Harry then John will be furious.

---

46 You see that we have the same string of symbols in each case! But we saw that Ex. 75 meant

It is not the case that (or: it's not true that) *if Mary is John's ex-wife and Mary is engaged to Harry, then John will be furious.*

While Ex. 76 meant

Mary is not John's ex-wife, and if Mary is engaged to Harry then John will be furious.

So the *same* string of symbols is capable of bearing two different meanings, depending on how it is boxed up! Clearly we *need* the boxes, or something like them in our symbolic notation, to punctuate the strings and avoid ambiguity. What exactly do the boxes do, to make this possible? Have another look at the two different readings of "~ p & q → r".

Ex. 75.

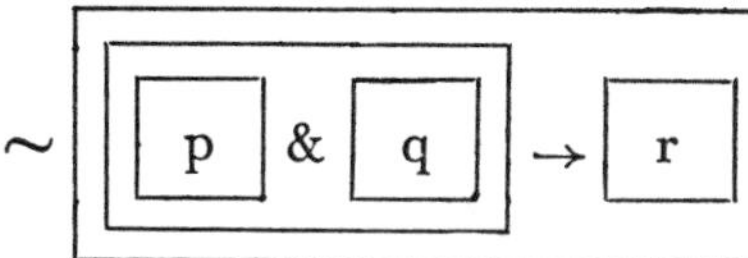

Ex. 76

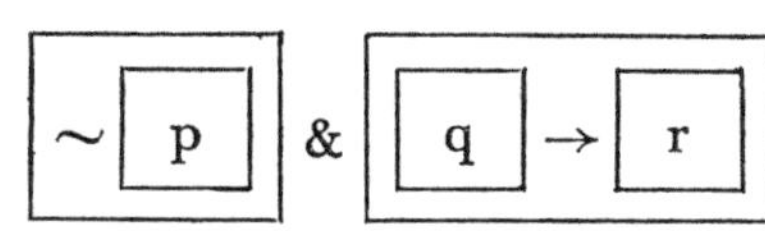

You can see that in each there is just *one* operator which is not inside any of the boxes. In Ex. 75 it is the left-hand most tilde—ringed below:

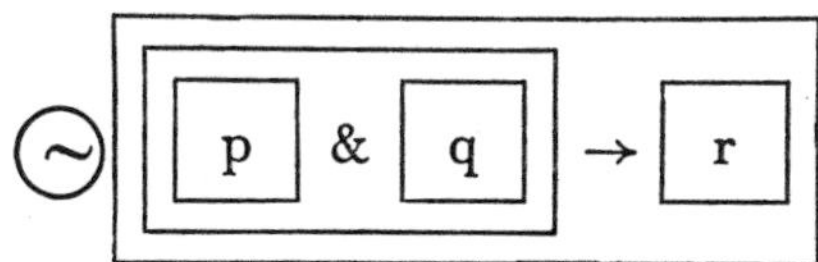

Which is it in Ex. 76? Ring the operator which is not inside any of the boxes in Ex. 76 below

Ex. 76

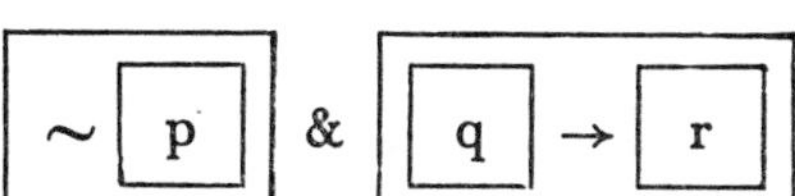

Ex. 75. ~ p & q → r
Ex. 76. ~ p & q → r

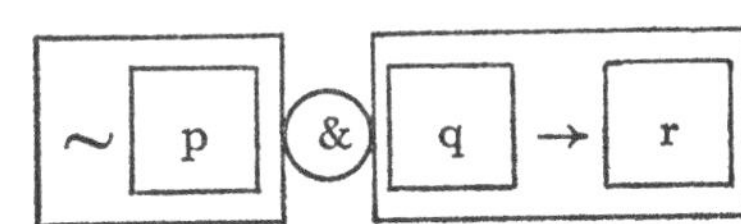

47 The operator which occurs outside all boxes is called the **main operator** of a formula. We indicate the main operator of a formula by labelling it (1), thus:

Main operator

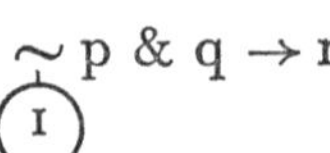

The main operator (or operator (1)) of a formula operates on the contents of the outermost box or boxes of a formula, considered as one sentence; and it determines what kind of formula the whole formula is. So far we have met six kinds of formulae:
(1) The sentential variable on its own such as

p

or

q

which we will call a **simple formula** or **simple sentence.**

Simple formula
Simple sentence

(2) The negation which states that something is *not* the case. So the basic form of the negation is "It is not the case that . . ." (which from now on we shall always abbreviate to "Not . . ."). Until this week all negations have been simple formulae plus the tilde, such as

~*p* (*Not p*).

(3) The conjunction, which states that *both* of two things are the case. So the basic form of the conjunction is "(Both) . . . and . . . " Until this week, all conjunctions have been simple formulae joined together by &, such as

p & *q* (*p and q*).

(4) The disjunction, which states that at least one and possibly both of two things are the case. So the basic form of the disjunction is "Either . . . or . . . (or both)". Until this week, all disjunctions have been simple formulae joined together by v, such as

p v *q* (*p or q*).

(5) The conditional, which states that *if* one thing is the case, *then* so is another. So the basic form of the conditional is "If . . . then . . ." Until this week, all conditionals have been simple formulae joined together by an arrow, such as

p → *q* (*if p, then q*)

(6) The **biconditional,** which states: *both* that if one thing is the case, then so is another; *and* that, if this other thing is the case, then so is the first. Again, until this week all biconditionals have been simple formulae joined together by ↔, such as

Biconditional

p ↔ *q*.

Since well-formed formulae containing operators are themselves (or more correctly: themselves stand for) sentences, they too can form negations, conjunctions, disjunctions, or conditionals and biconditionals, occupying the place that before this week has been occupied by sentential variables. Obviously this means that formulae containing more than one operator are possible. When there is more than one operator in a formula, the boxes determine whether one reads the formula as a whole negation, a conjunction, a disjunction, a conditional or a biconditional.

The main operator of

Ex. 75.

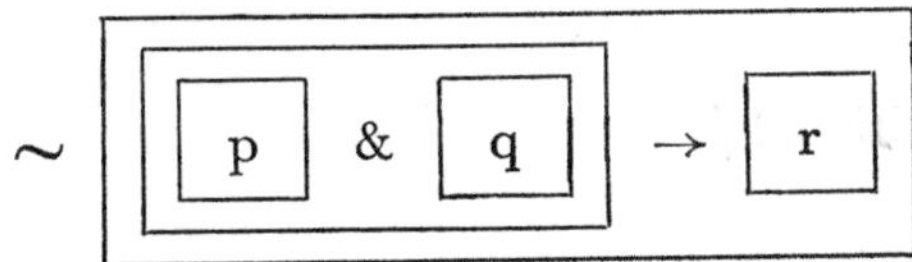

is ~. So Ex. 75 is a

simple formula / negation / conjunction / disjunction / conditional / biconditional?

---

48 The main operator of

Ex. 76

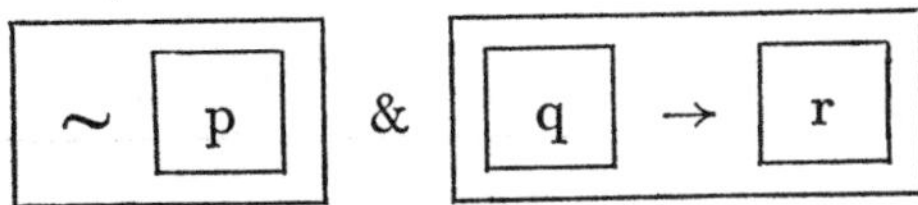

is &. So Ex. 76 is a

simple formula / negation / conjunction / disjunction / conditional / biconditional?

Ex. 75 is a negation: it says that the statement represented by the contents of the outermost box is *not* the case.

---

49 It is just the outermost box or boxes in a formula which serve to indicate the main operator. What about the other boxes? Look at the formula inside the outermost box of Ex. 75, i.e.

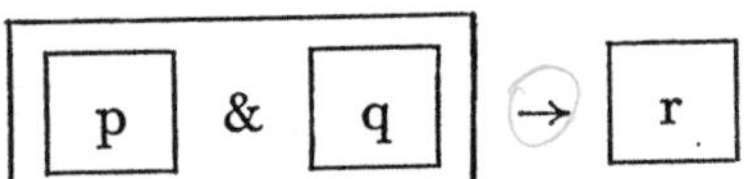

As you can see, this formula too has more than one operator—and again, there is just one operator in this formula, which occurs outside any of the boxes. Which is it? Draw a ring round it:

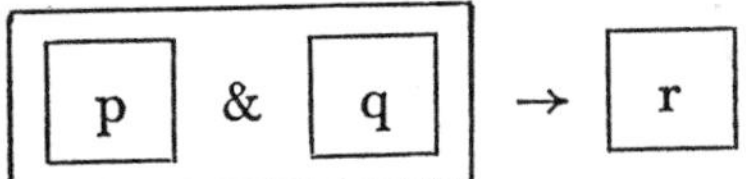

Ex. 76 is a conjunction: it says that *both* the statement represented by the contents of the outermost box to the left of the &, and the statement represented by the contents of the outermost box to the right of the &, are true.

---

50 We call this operator, operator (2). Operator (2) is the main operator of the formula on which operator (1) operates. The formula inside the outermost box of Ex. 75—i.e. the formula on which the operator (1) of Ex. 75 operates—is therefore a

simple sentence / negation / conjunction / disjunction / conditional / biconditional?

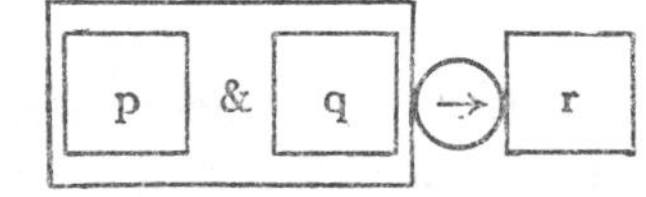

---

51 Now look inside the remaining boxes. What is inside the box to the right of the arrow in the last example?

Conditional

---

52 So the formula to the right of the arrow in this example is a

simple formula / negation / conjunction / disjunction / conditional / biconditional

r

---

53 Now look at the box to the *left* of the arrow in this example i.e.

[[p] & [q]]

Write out the formula it contains:

Simple formula

---

54 What is the main operator of this formula—the operator not contained in a box? Draw a ring round it:

[p] & [q]

[p] & [q]

---

55 We call this operator, operator (3). Operator (3) is the main operator of any formula on which operator (2) operates. So the formula whose main operator is operator (3) in Ex. 75 is a

simple formula / negation / conjunction / disjunction / conditional / biconditional?

[p] (&) [q]

---

56 (Notice that where there is only one operator in a formula, that operator still counts as the main one by the definition I have given this week.)

Now look at the box to the left of the & in this conjunction. Write out the formula it contains.

Conjunction

---

57 So the formula to the left of the & in this conjunction is a

simple formula / negation / conjunction / disjunction / conditional / biconditional?

p

---

58 Finally consider the contents of the last box: | q | , to the right of the & in the conjunction. Is the formula it contains a

simple formula / negation / conjunction / disjunction / conditional / biconditional?

Simple formula

---

59 So we can see that what the boxes do in a correctly-boxed formula is identify first the main operator of the whole formula and then in succession, the main operators of the shorter formulae out of which the original formula is made up. Different readings of the same string of symbols, which result in different meanings for the string, consist in different arrangements of the hierarchy of its operators. If we number the operators of the string ~ p & q → r like this:

Simple formula

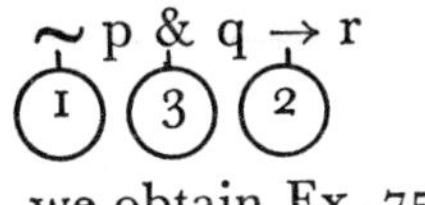

we obtain Ex. 75:

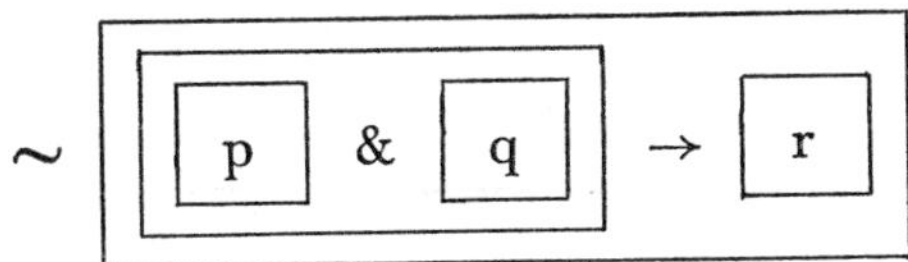

If we number the operators of the same string like this:

~ p & q → r
(2) (1) (2)

we obtain Ex. 76:

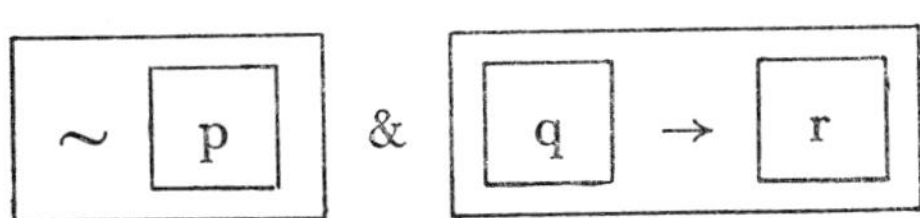

Notice that in Ex. 76, we have *two* operators labelled (2). This is because (a) operator (1) is & and therefore "takes" *two* boxes; (b) each of these boxes contains an operator. Thus, each of these operators occurs at the *same* level of the hierarchy of operators (i.e. inside the same number of boxes).

Our numbering of operators indicates their hierarchy: the numbers amount to exact instructions on how to box up a string. For example, a string with operators labelled like this:

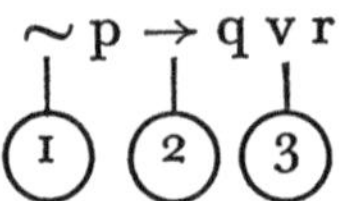

would be boxed up as follows:

Step 1. We put everything except operator (1) into a box. Since operator (1) is ~ and operates on a single sentence, we will need only one box:

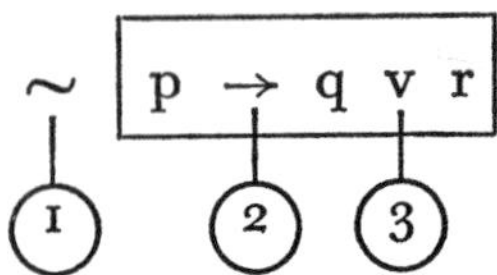

Step 2. Working inside the first box, we put everything except operator (2) into boxes. Since operator (2) is an arrow, and operates on two sentences at a time, we will need two boxes, one for the antecedent and one for the consequent of the conditional:

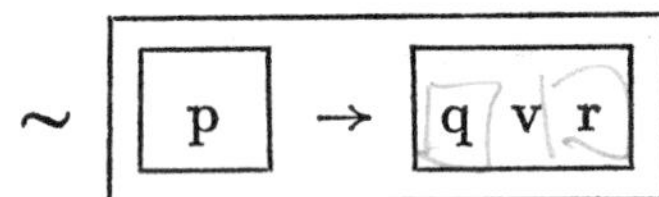

Step 3. Working inside the box that contains operator (3), we put everything except operator (3) into a box. Operator (3) is v. So how many boxes will we need?

one/two/three/none?

---

60 Complete step (3):

Two

61 Box the following string as indicated by the numbering:

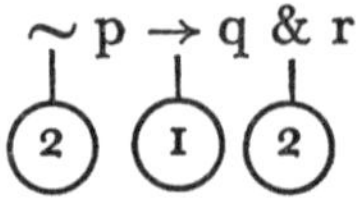

Step 1.

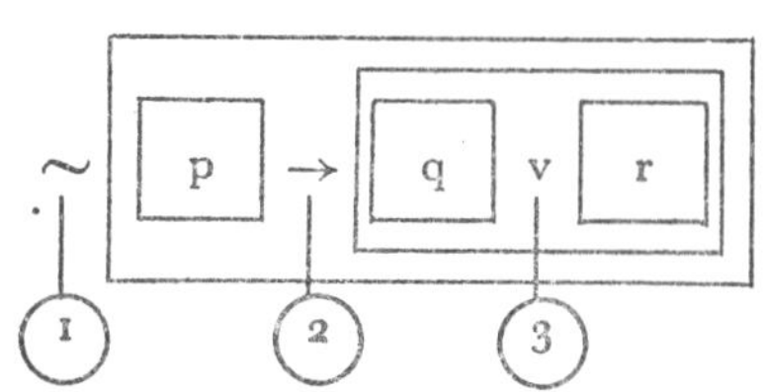

~p → q & r

62 *Step 2.*

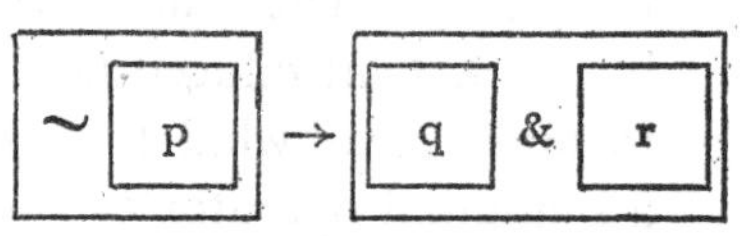

63 Box the following string as indicated by the numbering:

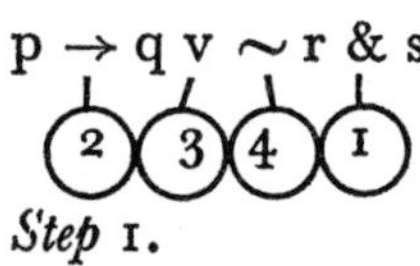

Step 1.

---

64 *Step 2.*

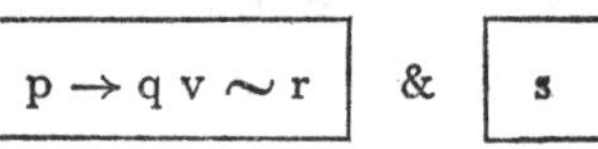

---

65 *Step 3.*

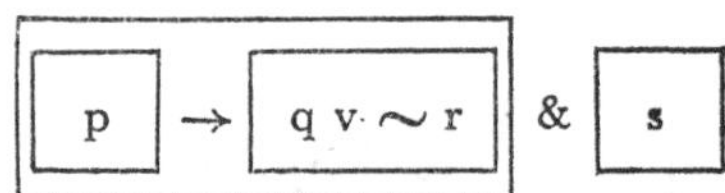

---

66 *Step 4.*

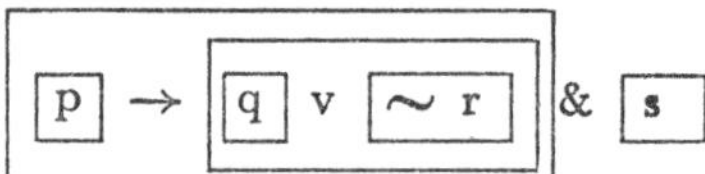

---

67 Box the following string as indicated by the numbering:

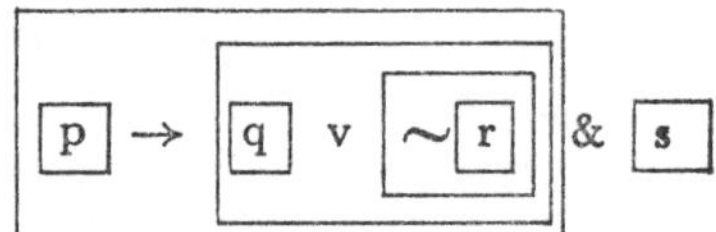

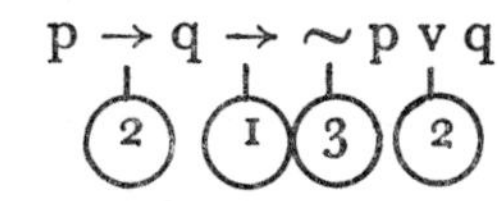

---

68 Obviously we must have something in our notation to indicate the hierarchy of operators, and do the work the boxes do, if we are to avoid ambiguity and confusion. In practice, boxes themselves are

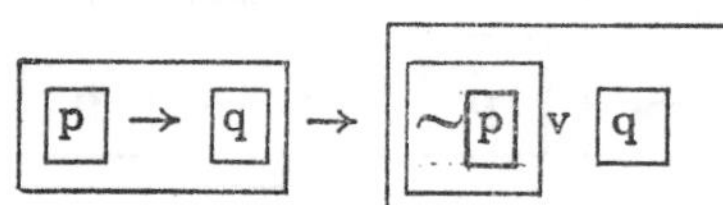

rather too unwieldly to use: they are difficult to draw quickly and take a lot of space, as you have probably realised yourself by now! What is normally used in their place is **brackets.**

Brackets

Brackets

Brackets are used for exactly the same purpose as we have been using boxes. The rules for their use are easily obtained if we bear this in mind. I introduced boxes at the beginning of this week in order to make clear what the scope of a sentential operator was. Now, a sentential operator can only operate on sentences; when I introduced the first box, which you remember occurred in this formula:

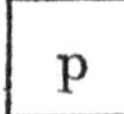

I said, "The box signifies a *sentence*". The sentential variable "p" stands for a sentence (in our example, for the sentence "Mary is John's ex-wife"), so it can go into a box. The next step was to consider the formula

p & q

I said of this: "This again is a whole new sentence, which can also be put into a sentence-box" thus

p & q

We stick to the same principle in using brackets: instead of enclosing each complete sentence in a box, we enclose each complete sentence in a pair of brackets. Instead of

p we write (p)

and instead of

p & q we write ((p) & (q))

The contents of any pair of brackets *must* be a complete sentence (in symbolic language, a wff); for brackets are used to indicate the scope of operators, and operators only operate on complete sentences (wffs). Operators operate on the *whole* of the contents of pairs of brackets outside which they occur, the contents of each pair of brackets being considered as one sentence (wff).

Replace the boxes in the following formula with brackets. (Be careful to check that you have the same number of left and right-hand brackets!) It is easiest to start from the innermost box and work outwards.

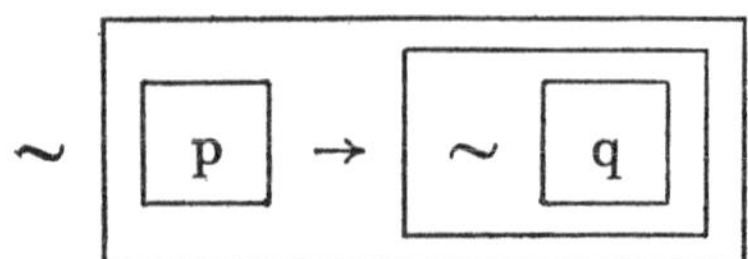

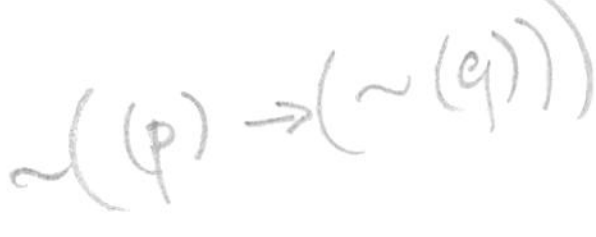

69 Replace the boxes in the following formula with brackets: $\sim((p) \rightarrow (\sim(q)))$

$$\boxed{\sim \boxed{p}} \rightarrow \boxed{\sim \boxed{q}}$$

---

70 This use of brackets exactly parallels the use I have been making of boxes: in effect, all we have done is remove the two horizontal edges of the boxes. The result certainly states unambiguously what each operator is meant to apply to, but—it may take you a little time to work it out! And that's the snag: all those brackets are visually very confusing. In fact not all of them are absolutely necessary to make clear the scope of each operator. For these brackets are being used just like boxes; and boxes when first introduced were partly used to indicate complete sentences. Hence the first box round the "p" in $(\sim(p)) \rightarrow (\sim(q))$

$$\sim \boxed{p}$$

But this formula *without* the box—i.e.

$$\sim p$$

is perfectly clear; there is no problem about the scope of the operator. The same would be true of the formula

$$p \rightarrow q.$$

But brackets or boxes are absolutely necessary in this formula, which contains two operators:

$$\sim p \rightarrow q$$

because the $\sim$ and the $\rightarrow$ appear to be, so to speak, *competing* for influence over the "p". Brackets are needed to indicate which wins —the $\sim$, thus:

$$(\sim p) \rightarrow q$$

or the $\rightarrow$, thus:

$$\sim(p \rightarrow q).$$

If we simply bracket the "p" and the "q", thus:

$$\sim(p) \rightarrow (q)$$

the string remains just as ambiguous as it was before; for *these* brackets, which contain only a sentential variable and no operator, only indicate that they contain a complete sentence; they do not help to delineate the scope of the operators. This is only achieved by the *other* pairs of brackets:

$$(\sim p) \rightarrow q$$

and

$$\sim(p \rightarrow q)$$

which do it by showing which symbols in the string are to be considered together.

So we can simplify our use of brackets by discarding those which contain only a sentential variable. Removing just these brackets from

$(\sim (p)) \rightarrow (\sim (q))$

we obtain

$(\sim p) \rightarrow (\sim q)$

which is still unambiguous, and a lot easier to read.
Remove the brackets containing only sentential variables from the following formula:

$\sim ((p) \rightarrow (\sim (q)))$.

---

71 Re-write the following formula without the brackets containing only sentential variables: $\sim (p \rightarrow (\sim q))$

$(p) \rightarrow ((q) \rightarrow (r))$.

---

72 Re-write the following formula without the brackets containing only sentential variables: $p \rightarrow (q \rightarrow r)$

$((p)\ \&\ (q))\ \mathrm{v}\ ((q) \rightarrow (p))$.

---

73 Re-write the following formula without the brackets containing only sentential variables $(p\ \&\ q)\ \mathrm{v}\ (q \rightarrow p)$

$(\sim (p)) \rightarrow ((\sim (q))\ \&\ (q))$.

---

74 Re-write the following formula without the brackets containing only sentential variables: $(\sim p) \rightarrow ((\sim q)\ \&\ q)$

$(\sim (p))\ \mathrm{v}\ ((q)\ \&\ (\sim (\sim (r))))$.

---

75 We can now summarize the five rules for the use of brackets: $(\sim p)\ \mathrm{v}\ (q\ \&\ (\sim (\sim r)))$

(1) Brackets are only necessary in strings (formulae) containing more than one operator.

(2) Every sentence containing more than one operator must be bracketed, in such a way that it is not ambiguous.

(3) Every pair of brackets must enclose a complete sentence (a well-formed formula).
(4) Single sentential variables are not bracketed.
(5) There must be an equal number of left-hand and right-hand brackets.

Here is a list of formulae. Some of them are correctly bracketed according to our five rules, others are incorrectly bracketed. Put a tick by the ones which are correctly bracketed and a cross by those which are incorrectly bracketed; and state which rule or rules the incorrect ones violate.

76

	Formula	x or ✓	Rules violated
a	$\sim$ (p)		
b	($\sim$ p)		
c	(p $\rightarrow$ q)		
d	$\sim$ (p $\rightarrow$ q)		
e	$\sim$ (p $\rightarrow$ q		
f	p & $\sim$ q		
g	p (v $\sim$ q)		
h	(p $\rightarrow$) $\sim$ q		
i	p v ($\sim$ q)		
j	p & $\sim$ (q)		
k	$\sim$ (p $\rightarrow$ ($\sim$ q)		
l	$\sim$ (p v ($\sim$ q))		
m	$\sim$ (p) & ($\sim$ q))		
n	$\sim$ (p $\rightarrow$ ($\sim$ q))		

---

77 Bracket the following string so that the ringed operator is the main one: remember the 5 bracketing rules!

$p \textcircled{\rightarrow} q \rightarrow r$

Correct: (d), (i), (l), (n)
Incorrect: (a) Rules 1 & 4; (b) 1; (c) 1; (e) 5; (f) 2; (g) 3; (h) 3; (j) 2 & 4; (k) 5; (m) 2 & 4 & 5

$p \rightarrow (q \rightarrow r)$

78 Bracket the following string so that the ringed operator is the main one:

$p \rightarrow q \textcircled{\rightarrow} r$

$(p \rightarrow q) \rightarrow r$

79 Bracket the following string so that the ringed operator is the main one:

$\textcircled{\sim} p \ \& \ q$

$\sim (p \ \& \ q)$

80 Bracket the following string so that the ringed operator is the main one:

$\sim p \textcircled{\vee} q$

$(\sim p) \vee q$

81 Bracket the following string so that ringed operator is the main one:

$\sim p \textcircled{\rightarrow} \sim q$

$(\sim p) \rightarrow (\sim q)$

Exercises on part IX—Brackets

A: Ring the main operator in the following formulae and state whether each is a negation or a conditional:

1. $\sim((\sim p) \rightarrow q)$
2. $p \rightarrow ((\sim q) \rightarrow r)$
3. $(\sim (p \rightarrow q)) \rightarrow r$
4. $\sim((p \rightarrow q) \rightarrow r)$
5. $(p \rightarrow (q \rightarrow r)) \rightarrow (q \rightarrow (p \rightarrow r))$
6. $\sim((p \rightarrow q) \rightarrow (q \rightarrow p))$.

B: Bracket the following strings as indicated by the numbering, and keeping the five bracketing rules:

1. $p \rightarrow \sim q \rightarrow r$
   Numbering: 1 2 3

2. $p \rightarrow \sim q \rightarrow r$
   Numbering: 2 3 1

3. $\sim p \ \& \sim q \vee r$
   Numbering: 1 2 3 4

4. $\sim p \ \& \sim q \vee r$
   Numbering: 2 1 2 3

5. $\sim p \ \& \sim q \vee r$
   Numbering: 3 2 3 1

6. $\sim p \ \& \sim q \vee r$.
   Numbering: 2 3 4 1

Answers

A:

1. $\textcircled{\sim}((\sim p) \rightarrow q)$; negation
2. $p\textcircled{\rightarrow}((\sim q) \rightarrow r)$; conditional
3. $(\sim (p \rightarrow q))\textcircled{\rightarrow}r$; conditional
4. $\textcircled{\sim}((p \rightarrow q) \rightarrow r)$; negation
5. $(p \rightarrow (q \rightarrow r))\textcircled{\rightarrow}(q \rightarrow (p \rightarrow r))$; conditional
6. $\textcircled{\sim}((p \rightarrow q) \rightarrow (q \rightarrow p))$; negation

B:

1. $p \rightarrow (\sim (q \rightarrow r))$
2. $(p \rightarrow (\sim q)) \rightarrow r$
3. $\sim (p \ \& \ (\sim (q \vee r)))$
4. $(\sim p) \ \& \ (\sim (q \vee r))$
5. $((\sim p) \ \& \ (\sim q)) \vee r$
6. $(\sim (p \ \& \ (\sim q))) \vee r$

ACKNOWLEDGEMENTS

Grateful acknowledgement is made to the following source for material used in this unit:

Hill & Wang for George Bernard Shaw, 'Censorship as a Police Duty' in *Platform and Pulpit*, ed. Dan H. Laurence, 1961.

HUMANITIES: A FOUNDATION COURSE

Introduction

1 Humanities and the Study of Civilization
2 The Yorubas of Nigeria
3 Technology, Society, Religion and the Arts: Some Questions
4 The Artist and Society

History

5 What History Is, and Why it is Important
6 Primary Sources
7 Basic Problems of Writing History
8 Common Pitfalls in Historical Writing

Literature

9 Introduction to Literature (Part I)
10 Introduction to Literature (Part II)

Art

11 Introduction to Art (Part I)
12 Introduction to Art (Part II)

Music

13 Introduction to Music (Part I)
14 Introduction to Music (Part II)

Form and Meaning

15 Form and Meaning (Part I)
16 Form and Meaning (Part II)

Socrates

17 18 Which was Socrates?

What is a Gospel?

19 20 What is a Gospel?

Vasari

21 22 Giorgio Vasari: Renaissance Art-Critic and Art-Historian

Hamlet

23 24 Shakespeare's *Hamlet*

Descartes

25 26 Descartes: The Father of Modern Philosophy

Mendelssohn

27 Mendelssohn's Rediscovery of Bach (Part I)
28 Mendelssohn's Rediscovery of Bach (Part II)

Industrialisation

29 30 The Industrialisation Process:
Part I: The Railway: The Evolution of the Machine
Part II: How the Railway System was Created
Part III: Glasgow: Transport, Mechanisation and Society
31 The Debate on Industrialisation
32 Is Man a Machine?
33 34 Art and Industry
35 36 D. H. Lawrence's *The Rainbow*

L1 Introduction to Logic (Parts I–IX)
L2 Introduction to Logic (Parts X–XVIII)